Where Wrestling Lives

THE PRO WRESTLING VAULT

VOLUME 1

Vinny Berry

CREDITS:

Written by Vinny Berry
Photography by Jon-Paul LeBlanc
Produced by Wrestleville & WOHW
Layouts - Wrestleville
Cover Art - Iron Skull Productions
www.wrestleville.com

WARNING:

WELCOME TO A CELEBRATION OF PRO WRESTLING

**THE PRO WRESTLING VAULT
VOLUME 1**

Printed in the USA

ADAM PEARCE

Photo by Wrestleville - Vinny Berry

NWA WORLD HEAVYWEIGHT CHAMPION

1ST: September 1, 2007 - August 2, 2008
2ND: September 2, 2008 - October 25,2008
3RD: March 14, 2010 - March 6, 2011
4TH: July 31, 2011 - April 8, 2012
5TH: July 21, 2012 - October 27, 2012

CODY

Jon-Paul Le Blanc - 4 Corners Photography

WWE INTERCONTINENTAL CHAMPION
1ST: 8-9-2011 - 1-4-2012
2ND: 4-29-2012 - 5-20-2012

RING OF HONOR CHAMPION
6-23-2017 - 12-15-2017

NWA WORLD HEAVYWEIGHT CHAMPION
9-1-2018 - 10-20-2018

JAZZ

Jon-Paul Le Blanc - 4 Corners Photography

WWE WOMEN'S WORLD CHAMPION
1ST: February 4, 2002 - May 13, 2002
2ND: April 27, 2003 - June 30, 2003

NWA WOMEN'S WORLD CHAMPION
September 16, 2016 - April 22, 2019

TABLE OF CONTENTS

NWA CHAMPIONS

Jon-Paul Le Blanc - 4 Corners Photography

NWA's Finest in 2016 - (Left to right) **Greg Anthony, Big Ramp,** (Manager) **Rob Conway, Amber O'Neal, Jax Dane, Matt Riveria, Tim Storm, & Steve Anthony**

FOREWARD

I think I first came across Vincent Berry about five years ago. He wrote me a nice letter and said he liked some of the books that I had worked on at WOHW.com. He then wanted to know if I would check out some of his articles for feedback. He's smart. How can you say "no" after someone babyfaces you like that? Then, he sent me a couple of links, and I looked at them in due time. I was actually very surprised. His articles read very well. The stories were nicely researched and not like much of what I had seen online. You could tell he took the articles very seriously and wanted readers to really learn something from his research. Just like me, he likes to keep the legend alive.

There is something to be said for somebody who writes from an area of passion to the highest degree, and you can absolutely see that in Vinny's writings. His work is just meticulous, and if you were reading this right now, I believe you'll really be in for a treat when I'm done putting him over.

After a few years of our initial confrontation, I started nagging Vinny to take on a book project for me when I was kind of busy doing some of my own. I was surprised when he kayfabed me and acted like writing a biography was not the area he wanted to go in at that time.

However, little did I know that he was working me - he was talking to Lance Von Erich and working on a top-secret book project of his own! In the spirit of paying it forward, I offered to help him however way I could. I know when I first got my start I was totally blind on how to actually put a book together. Vinny was also in the same situation, and accepted.

I was on a road trip, and Vinny called me to pick my brain. I gave him so much information I think I blew his mind. Couple that with the fact that he has a short term memory not unlike the fish from Nemo, and it is safe to say that that one phone call was not the last.

This is totally fine now, and I've enjoyed actually switching the roles. Recently, I am now finding myself passing on information to newer writers so that he/she can get their information out there to the fans. This is super rewarding to me.

If you are a wrestling history buff you will totally enjoy this work. I would guess that it would be great to read all of the stories of The Pro Wrestling Vault at your leisure - perhaps before bed, or even better how I believe the author intended it, sitting on the crapper... This truly is where the best learning occurs in my house.

Either way - nothing but well wishes out to Vinny for another great contribution to the wrestling community and fans everywhere.

Kenny Casanova
WOHW.com

PREFACE

After years of covering the sports of boxing and MMA, I wanted to write about the first sport that got my attention. In 2017, I started a website called Wrestleville. On that space, I post stories of people who work and have worked in professional wrestling. The people I write about are a mix of veteran and up and coming wrestlers.

Since the website's inception, and over time, I began to make several contacts and friends in the wrestling industry. One of those people is Jon-Paul LeBlanc, a wrestling photographer from New Orleans, Louisiana. We became instant friends and when I needed a particular picture of a certain wrestler, he sent it my way. I have always been impressed by the amount of pictures he has taken at the multiple events over the course of years. I can easily get lost going through his collection.

On almost every weekend Jon-Paul can be found at a wrestling show in his home state, or in Texas, Mississippi, and Alabama. You can say he has the Gulf Coast region of the United States covered when it comes to photographing the sport. After I finished my first book, "Lance by Chance: Wrestling as a Von Erich," I began to research my next project. The story I wanted to tell was how pro wrestling had been affected by the Covid pandemic. After hitting a few dead-ends, I switched gears. Since Jon-Paul and I collectively had a massive amount of stories and pictures, we decided to combine our efforts.

Trying to come up with a name for this project was not easy. Since almost all the photos that we have are from the Gulf Coast region we wanted that name in the title. However, we did not want our audience to think that was what the entire book was about. In this publication we are also presenting a wide range of stories that include well-known legends and athletes on the rise from all over the United States.

Sadly, some of the wrestlers in this book have passed away. We are confident that the work that they accomplished inside the ring will not be forgotten. Jon-Paul and I are privileged to share this material with you. The date listed on the top of the page is when the stories were posted on the website and the photos were taken. Our goal is to provide a platform where we can preserve wrestling moments, so they do not fade away. We believe you will enjoy The Pro Wrestling Vault Volume. 1.

Vinny Berry

wrestleville.com
lancebychance.com

VORDELL WALKER – APRIL 12, 2017

Jon-Paul Le Blanc - 4 Corners Photography

Since 2001, Vordell Walker has been making his presence known in the sport of professional wrestling. The six-foot, 225-pound wrestler is a firefighter during the day, but by night, he is setting the ring ablaze when going after his opponents. Voodoo Wrestling, AML, NWA Ring Warriors, PWX, and Main Event, are a list of promotions that Walker has wrestled for throughout his career. He has also done some work with TNA, Ring of Honor, and the WWE. For some wrestlers, to be in front of a large WWE crowd might cause some anxiety, but not for Walker. He was right at home when he worked against Titus O'Neal and Tyler Breeze in a couple of dark matches at Wrestlemania 25. To this day, those memories have remained with him.

"We all get into the sport with aspirations of making it to that level. Some of us make it and some of us don't," Walker explained. "If you don't make it in the WWE, it's not always a lack of talent. It's just the nature of the game."

For years, when Walker lived in Georgia, he traveled to places like Florida, North Carolina, Massachusetts, Texas, California, and Mexico, just to wrestle. It did not matter how far it was. There were times that his colleagues gave him a hard time for going everywhere and not staying in one place to wrestle. Despite their criticism, Walker did it anyway.

"I think it's necessary. To be great, you have to step out of your comfort zone." Walker said. "You just can't sit in one area and expect to grow as a wrestler, a performer, or whatever the case may be."

In 2015, Walker was wrestling for AML in North Carolina. It was there he found that he had great chemistry when he worked in the ring with King Shane Williams. Williams, who is always accompanied by his valet Queen Taylor; never backed down from Walker's challenge. The two wrestlers had a heated feud that lasted for several months. Fans came out to watch them settle their score every time they stepped into battle. The conflict between the two men got so serious that AML put them against each other in a "Best of 5 Series" to see who would reign supreme. At the end of the sequence of matches , Williams came out on top, but that did not mean that he got the best of Walker. No one knew that Walker was just waiting to catch his foe off guard.

During a match Williams had against then Champion Papadon for the AML Title in Winston-Salem, Walker's diabolical plan unfolded. After 20 minutes had passed in the action, the King looked as if he was going to capture the championship belt. Then, out of nowhere Walker entered the venue and interfered in the contest. Due to Walker's intrusion the referee stopped the match and Papadon retained his title. But nothing was able to stop Walker from continuing his assault on Williams. Those in attendance were shocked by what they witnessed. After several minutes went by, the altercation was eventually broken up by AML officials, but not before Walker sought his revenge. Tracy Myers, the Owner of AML, was so upset that he announced over the microphone that Walker was fired from the promotion. Not since that day has Walker been back to wrestle for the promotion. If the holder of the company sticks to his guns, he never will.

"I think my point was proven," Walker stated. "When one door closes another one opens, but I left my mark there at AML."AML was a wrestling promotion where Walker might have left his mark, but he has also had some matches in his career that were special to him. One of those specific moments came when

Walker went against a wrestling legend, 2 Cold Scorpio. The match took place in 2012 for USA Pro Wrestling in Orlando, Florida.

"He was a little older, but you couldn't tell," Walker continued. "He was smooth as ice and our match flowed well."

Scorpio's in-ring style and experience in the sport, can easily make him a wealth of knowledge for anyone who wants to learn from him. Walker took full advantage of the opportunity that was in front of him.

"We worked more of a Japanese style of a match. There was striking, there was drama, and it picked up when it needed to pick up," Walker added. "Anytime I have wrestled someone with that type of background, it has always been a beautiful chess game on the mat."

2 Cold Scorpio wrestled for nearly 30 years with companies like WCW, ECW, WWE, and he has also spent some time in the New Japan Pro Wrestling promotion.

Walker is dedicated to the sport. The time that he has invested into his passion has paid off for him. Match after match, in addition to his extensive time spent on the road has proved his dedication for the business, even when some people have doubted him.

"When I was young I told people that I was going to be a wrestler and they treated it as if it was a pipe dream for me," Walker said. "It was just something I always wanted to do since I was a kid, and now I'm doing it."

Jon-Paul Le Blanc - 4 Corners Photography

Vordell Walker vs. John Saxon

CHAZ TAYLOR – APRIL 13, 2017

Wrestleville – Vinny Berry

Few people can say that they have been actively wrestling for 30 years. It is not a sport that is kind to one's body. For someone to be able to stick with it for that long, they have to love it. For Chaz Taylor of Houston, Texas, he does.

The 46-year-old is the son of wrestler Tugboat Taylor. To provide for his family, Tugboat wrestled professionally. As a teenager and as long as Chaz kept his grades up in school, he was allowed to go on the road with his Father. While at the matches, Chaz took the wrestler's jackets from the ring to the dressing room. Sometimes a referee did not show up and Chaz had the honor to do that duty for the night. Then there were the nights that luck was really on Taylor's side.

"Sometimes I was told a wrestler didn't show up," Taylor recalled. "Do you have your boots and are you ready to wrestle?" "It kind of just went on from there."

With his father in the business, he already had his trainer. It was not long before Taylor was stepping inside the ring regularly and wrestling full time. The Father and Son might have shared their love for the business, but due to the significant contrast in size between the two, their wrestling styles were very different from each other. That difference helped Chaz to find his path.

"Dad was a big guy and I was a small guy. So we didn't use the same ring moves," Taylor explained. "I had to look at wrestlers like the Rock N' Roll Express, The Fantastic's, The Cheetah Kid, and Jeff Jarrett. I learned a lot from them."

Taylor's use of the ropes and his ability to use his dexterity to his advantage made for several exciting high-flying stunts. His style often made the fans stand to their feet. His wrestling abilities were getting him noticed.

Traveling on the road always meant going to new and different places. Wrestling took Chaz all over the world to countries like Japan and Mexico. He has also worked in several promotions across the United States including, World Class Championship Wrestling, The National Wrestling Alliance, Total Non- Stop Action, World Championship Wrestling, Extreme Championship Wrestling, and The Global Wrestling Federation.

Chaz's time with the Global Wrestling Federation between 1990 and 1995, offered him a great deal of television exposure. It was there where he cut his teeth in the business and grew as a wrestler. Taylor did not find out how important that period of his life was until a few years later until he was working with the WWF.

"Christian, Edge, and the Hardy Boys came up to me in the dressing room and thanked me," Taylor continued. "They told me that they used to watch me and study my moves so they could create their own. They were thanking me! How cool is that?"

Chris Adams, Steve Austin, Shawn Michaels, Rod Price, and The Undertaker are a shortlist of people that Taylor has learned from along the way. His positive attitude and unique perspective on life, have allowed him to learn from just about everybody he has worked with. One wrestler that will remain in Taylor's memory for the rest of his life is Owen Hart. Taylor worked with the WWF when they took their tour through the Southern states. The two men wrestled against each other in the mid-'90s in cities throughout Texas and Oklahoma. It was around the same time that Owen and his brother Bret were having their wrestling feud.

"Wrestling Owen was like dancing the waltz because we always knew where the other guy was in the ring," Taylor added. "By the time we were done, we both wished we had more time because it so much fun."

On May 23, 1999, Owen Hart fell 78 feet to his death while being lowered into the ring with a harness and grapple line at a pay-per-view wrestling event in Kansas City, Missouri. The news of Hart's death traveled fast and it shocked everyone. Family, friends, wrestlers, and fans were heartsick. The wrestling business did not just lose a great wrestler, it lost a great person.

"He was a big loss, not just because of his talent, but he kept the locker room light-hearted and fun," Taylor sighed. "He was a prankster and he made sure we had fun during the stressful times on the road."

Sadness, triumphs, disappointments, and injuries, were all things that Taylor has had to deal with through his long career. With all the things that the wrestling business and his opponents could throw at him, through it all he prevailed. Taylor's reputation in the sport is widespread. Many schools and promotions have brought him out to do seminars and classes to teach the up-and-coming wrestlers what he has learned throughout his entire career.

"I'm happy to spread the knowledge and I'm happy to take the next generation and teach them right from wrong," Taylor expressed. "There are a lot of good trainers out there but sometimes the guys need to hear the same thing differently from someone else."

After achieving veteran wrestler status, Taylor's ideas for his business plan are changing. He is still wrestling and taking selective dates, but he is exploring other opportunities. Throughout the years of his wrestling career, he has done commercials, stunt work, extra work, and small parts in several movies. Chaz has also been in several music videos with artists like Coolio and ZZ Top. Next month Taylor is awaiting the release of a sitcom show that he stars in called "Suplex, Duplex, Complex." It is an 80's wrestling comedy that features the lives of two wrestling tag teams living next door to each other. Todd Rohal directs the show, and it recently won an award at this year's SXSW Movie & Music Festival in Austin, Texas. The skills that Taylor will need to be successful as an actor are all things that he has already perfected during his extensive wrestling career.

"Wrestling is one of the most unappreciative art forms there is," Taylor said. "With doing the movies and acting, I don't have to wake up so sore every morning."

Photo by Wrestleville

Chaz Taylor - 2012

Jon-Paul Le Blanc - 4 Corners Photography

Chaz Taylor - 2014

DAMIEN WAYNE – APRIL 14, 2017

Jon-Paul Le Blanc - 4 Corners Photography

Toughness, skill, heart, and determination are just a few attributes that wrestler Damien Wayne possesses. No one can take away his passion for the sport of wrestling. The three-time former National Wrestling Alliance, National Heavyweight Champion grew up in Virginia and he was exposed to the Crockett's Mid Atlantic Wrestling Promotion. There might have been other wrestling programs that he had watched on television, but nothing could replace his affection for the NWA.

"Back in the day, that company and that championship belt, no matter who held it was always been regarded at the highest level," Wayne explained. "All the places it has been defended and the legacy behind that belt is incredible. I know today that it doesn't mean what it used to, but those three letters still mean something to me."

From the age of seven, Wayne was a huge wrestling fan and it was always something that he was interested in pursuing. However, he was bit by the baseball bug and discovered that it was a sport he was pretty good at. Wayne played baseball through high school, but a shoulder injury eliminated any hopes of a future with the game. By the age of 25, Wayne was married and was busy raising children with his wife. Though his love for wrestling never went away, it was not the priority he was focusing on. Then one day in 2001, he discovered Virginia Championship Wrestling through the Internet.

"It was funny because they ran shows for three years two blocks from where I worked for 14 years. I never knew they were running shows there," Wayne said. "I emailed them, but I was 30 years old and 166 pounds, so being a wrestler was pretty much out of the question at that point in my head, but I thought I could be a referee or be on the ring crew. I just wanted to be a part of it."

It was in November of that same year when Wayne reached out to the promotion that is now Vanguard Championship Wrestling. As luck would have it, the promotion was going to start a school at the turn of the year, and Wayne had made up his mind that he was going to attend. This is where his toughness and determination came into play. Wayne showed up at the wrestling school with 26 other potential students, but within a couple of days, the size of the class was much different.

"I was the only one left. They all dropped like flies," Wayne laughed. "Nothing is going to kill my passion for professional wrestling. I have had some things happen to me over the years that the normal wrestler would have quit over, but I truly have a passion for the sport."

Wayne also has a strong passion for the NWA, and a desire to win the company's championship belt. Throughout his career, Wayne has had a handful of title opportunities. Though he has come close to winning the prestigious strap, fulfilling his ultimate dream has eluded him. By not achieving his dream, Wayne has been left frustrated and disappointed. In his second attempt to gain the title from former Champion Adam Pearce, both wrestlers exhausted every bit of energy that was in their bodies. Wayne and Pearce were fighting with purpose and fury, one man wanted to win the belt and the other man wanted to keep it. Pearce was not going to let Wayne take it away from him, at least without him having to work or die for it.

In the end, it looked as if Wayne had won the title when he pinned Pearce in the middle of the ring. The fans and Wayne thought history had been made and for a brief moment, Pearce thought his NWA title reign had come to an end. The fans went wild, and the guest presenter, former WWE Diva Sunny, brought the belt into the ring and awarded Wayne with it. Wayne was holding the belt in his hands thinking he achieved his life-long dream. Within moments, reality set in when it was brought to the referee's attention that the time limit of the match expired right before the official was able to get the third count on the pin.

"Knowing that I had to give the belt back hurt, but just having my name associated with that title is an accomplishment," Wayne confirmed. "That's what I grew up on. I went to the Hampton Arena and the Norfolk Scope so many times to watch Flair and Dusty wrestle for that belt, I have to admit it got to me."

It got to him because he loves the sport of wrestling and he understands what the NWA Title means to the sport. Damien Wayne has the heart of a champion and the determination to do what it takes to win. Wayne is a wrestler that his competitors need to watch out for, and someone they should fear. Wayne's dream of winning the NWA World Heavyweight Championship did not begin when he started wrestling in 2001. His dream of becoming Champion of the World started when he was seven years old.

Jon-Paul Le Blanc - 4 Corners Photography
Damien Wayne kicking Rodney Mack - April 3, 2017

TIM STORM – APRIL 15, 2017

Jon-Paul Le Blanc - 4 Corners Photography

Professional wrestler Tim Storm understands the tradition and what it means to be the National Wrestling Alliance World Heavyweight Champion. After being in the business for 20 years and having multiple shots with various Champions throughout his career, he finally achieved his lifelong goal. On October 21, 2016, Tim won the coveted belt from then Champion Jax Dane in Sherman, Texas.

Harley Race, Ric Flair, Dusty Rhodes, and the Funk Brothers are just a shortlist of some of the phenomenal wrestlers that have ever stepped inside the squared circle and have worn the NWA belt around their waist. Those names and many others will go down in the history books forever as being some of the best wrestlers in the sport. Tim Storm's name will also be in there.

"I am very proud to be a part of that, but I would never go down that list and say I can match up with any of those guys because those guys are legends," Tim Storm beamed. "The legacy that I want to leave behind is that I do deserve to be on that list, and I do deserve to be the World Champion. To a certain degree, I have already proven that."

When Storm stepped into the ring with Dane last fall, after having several failed attempts against the six-foot, four-inch, 300-pound powerhouse, Tim thought it could have been his last shot. Storm's dream of ever winning the prominent gold and leather strap was fading. Dane, who had held the championship for over

400 days, had fought the best in the business, match after match, as the NWA Champion has historically done since its inception in 1948.

"This is how amazing of a champion he is. He didn't have to give me another title shot. He already had beaten me three other times," Storm acknowledged. "He was an incredible champion in every aspect. He represented the NWA very well and he's a class act."

When you are the NWA World Heavyweight Champion, you travel the world. Storm traveled to Japan in February with the championship belt in tow. Traditionally, Japan has a rich heritage with the National Wrestling Alliance, and the belt that represents the company is a symbolic reminder of wrestling excellence. Storm's opponent was Ryota Hama, a very well-known local fighter who has MMA and Sumo wrestling experience. Hama stands five foot, nine inches but weighs nearly 500 pounds. Hama's size made it very difficult for Storm to prepare for.

"Traditional wrestling just doesn't work with a guy like that because I couldn't get my arms around the man," Storm commented. "I am normally the power guy. My game is to take my power to my opponent, but someone like that you are not going to be able to push them around."

Having to deal with the size advantage was one thing, but Tim knew that he was coming into his opponent's homeland. Strom expected to be treated like the out-of-town visitor, but he witnessed something different when he made his way from the curtain to the ring.

"When I walked out to the arena floor the fans started chanting NWA because of the history that the promotion has over there. The people of Japan respect the NWA," Storm exclaimed. "It wasn't that they were booing him by any means. I knew my role. The truth is that they cheered for us both."

As Storm expected, the wrestling match was not technical at all. Storm's offense quickly become his defense. Tim's main goal was not to be a victim of his opponent's girth. Early on, the Champion made his presence known by landing hard stiff punches to Hama's face.

"I was very physical, I threw a lot of punches, kicks, and forearms and I just tried to wear him down. My goal was to get him off his feet so he wouldn't be able to get back up," Storm responded. "I knew the longer the match lasted because of my conditioning, that I would have the advantage."

As the two men were attempting to deliver brain busters to each other, Hama lost his balance. Storm took advantage of the situation by hooking his legs, pulling him down to the mat, and wrapping Hama up for the pin and the victory.

"It was a unique match, but I knew who I was going in there with," Storm replied. "But how do you practice for a guy that's almost 500 pounds with an MMA and Sumo wrestling skill set? There are not too many people out there like that to practice with."

With his first overseas title defense out of the way, Storm returns to the United States where several top-notch wrestlers are waiting in line to have their turn for a title shot. Matt Riviera, Damien Wayne, Mike Beadle, Rob Conway, and Andrew Anderson, are just a handful of competitors that Storm could face in the upcoming weeks and months.

"There is a rich talent pool out there and potentially every single one of those guys could be a World Champion," Storm added. "But along those same lines, I don't expect to lose the title."

A few Facebook posts have eluded that the President of the NWA, Bruce Tharpe, might be having thoughts of Storm defending his title to Kazushi Miyamoto. Currently, Miyamoto is one-half of the NWA Tag Team Champions. If that were to happen, Storm will gladly defend his belt here or back over in Miyamoto's home country of Japan.

"I don't ever go into a match thinking that I am going to lose. I have a lot of confidence in myself," Storm stated. "I have nothing but respect for Miyamoto, but if I get in the ring with him I am going to beat him. I am the NWA World Heavyweight Champion and there is no one better than me in the business right now."

TIM STORM - 2014

Jon-Paul Le Blanc - 4 Corners Photography

NWA WORLD HEAVYWEIGHT CHAMPION
October 21, 2016 - December 9, 2017

GREG ANTHONY – APRIL 16, 2017

Jon-Paul Le Blanc - 4 Corners Photography

Greg Anthony is called the "Golden Boy" for one reason and one reason only. When he started wrestling 17 years ago, he was destined for championship glory. The man from Dyersburg, Tennessee gained notoriety while wrestling with Tradition Championship Wrestling between 2010 and 2013. No one can discount the fact that he has held nearly 80 different titles throughout his career from all over the United States.
Anthony has also held the NWA Mid-South Unified Champion six different times. However, no accomplishment might be sweeter than knowing that he has held the NWA National Heavyweight Title on three different occasions throughout 2016.

"It was a big year," Anthony exclaimed. "The competition was tough."

When you are the NWA National Champion, you are wrestling against some of the toughest and the biggest names in the business. It might just be one of the most prestigious wrestling belts there is next to the North American Title and the NWA World's Heavyweight Championship. Men who have stepped through the ropes and hoisted the National belt in the air include wrestlers such as Ron Garvin, Mr. Wrestling II, Dusty Rhodes, The Spoiler, Tully Blanchard, and The Masked Superstar. The list of names goes on and on with some of the best wrestlers that have ever laced up a pair of boots.

"It's humbling because a lot of those guys like Tully

Blanchard and the Masked Superstar are the guys that I have looked up to while I was growing up," Anthony reflected. "Those guys are amazing and to have my name etched in stone with them and that title, is humbling."

It was a chilly, wet, and rainy night on November, 19th 2016 when Anthony defended his NWA National Title in Gallatin, Tennessee to a man who is no stranger to the belt, Damien Wayne. Wayne had worn it proudly twice before that night throughout different times in his career.

"He's tough as nails. He is an old school guy like me and we beat the hell out of each other," Anthony stated. "He is as legit as legit can be."

Wayne was legit that night in North Central Tennessee, so legit that he ended up defeating Anthony and leaving him feeling very close in comparison to the weather outside. For the third time in one year, Anthony let the belt slip from his hands. He wondered whether he would get another shot to wrestle for his once-coveted championship. Anthony was familiar with his opponent, but that was the very first time that he went up against Wayne, the wrestler who has been referred to as the "Mid-Atlantic Bad Ass."

"I worked all year to build the National Title back up," Anthony exasperated. "To lose it was a tough pill to swallow."

The Golden Boy was taken to his limit. Not only was 2016 a great year for him as far as accomplishments went, but challenging in other aspects. His arch-rival and wrestling manager Christopher White has vowed to eliminate Greg Anthony from the sport.

"He showed up at the beginning of 2016 out of nowhere. He grew up in Dyersburg too and wanted to be a part of wrestling, but every time he mentioned wrestling my name was brought up," Anthony grumbled. "He has a rich Uncle in New York that is footing the bill and White's goal is to get me out of professional wrestling."

Some of the guns for hire that White brought in to try and defeat Anthony have been John Saxon, Rodney Mack, Wild Bill, and Mustang Mike. They were unable to get the job done, but the punishment that they delivered to the "Golden Boy" might have been enough to leave him vulnerable for Wayne's victory.

Anthony thought he was going to have his chance to take care of White for good last year when the two men squared off in a "Street Fight" style wrestling match. White claims he did not sign a waiver before the match took place and he threatened to sue the NWA. After dealing with all the legal issues that came from that ordeal, White has now been promoted to Chairman of the Championship Committee. Since then, White has formed a stable of wrestlers he calls "The Office." The Office includes White's bodyguard Jamal Soul along with wrestlers Jacob Edwin and The Posse, a tag team that features Simon Reed and Mr. Chris.

"The Posse had been fan favorites for 11 years in this area and now they have turned their backs on the people and jumped me," Anthony huffed. "They are running rough shot all over the Mid-South."

The Golden Boy may have his hands full while dealing with White and his henchmen, but there may be some things that his enemies do not know about him. Anthony has been mentored by one of the best wrestling technicians in the sport, Bobby Eaton one half of Jim Cornett's famed Midnight Express. The two met each other in 2009 and they formed a tag team called "Midnight Gold." Together they were unstoppable and they left an impression on the wrestling fans in the South. Their opponents knew the duo meant business and the ring was their workplace. Anthony is very grateful to have had the opportunity to wrestle with Eaton for two years.

"He was one of my favorite wrestlers growing up and then I ended up being his tag team partner, it was amazing," Anthony grinned. "It was educational, but at the same time it was a confidence booster for me because Bobby told everyone that I was the captain of the team."

Even though Anthony worked with Eaton near the tail end of his career, there were moments during their matches when Anthony caught a glimpse of the magic that made Bobby Eaton so special inside the squared circle.

"Every once in a while when we were tagging together, when I looked over in that corner it was like 1986 all over again," Anthony recalled. "There was no way Bobby Eaton was going to be the weak link in a match. I tagged him in and he went at it."

The lessons and small details that Eaton passed on to the "Golden Boy" about the art of wrestling were valuable. Anthony credits "Beautiful Bobby" for the road that he is currently on in his career today. Years of hard work and all the beatings are high prices that many have paid in the wrestling game. Not everyone in the dressing room is guaranteed success in a business that takes more than muscles and sequins sewed on a jacket to succeed.

"I believe that I was put on this earth to be in professional wrestling. It was just something that spoke to me personally and I have a great aptitude for it," Anthony mentioned. " You don't have to explain every little detail of the why's and the how's to me. That was always something that I just got."

Jon-Paul Le Blanc - 4 Corners Photography
Greg Anthony wrestling Ricky Morton in 2014

2017 PWHF INDUCTION – APRIL 24, 2017

The big blue building in Wichita Falls, Texas, is the home of the Pro Wrestling Hall of Fame and Museum. You will not only see event posters, ring attire, and an assortment of memorabilia; you will also see all the history that has been created in the sport.

"It is so important to keep the Hall of Fame and this museum alive because it tells the history of wrestling," Pro Wrestling Hall of Fame President of the Board of Directors, Johnny Mantell said. "It tells Vince's story, but it also tells the story of Killer Karl Kox, Dickie Murdoch, and those kinds of guys. If they were alive they would out wrestle the guys of today without even trying."

The month of May is a special time of year for the Pro Wrestling Hall of Fame. Starting on Thursday, May 18th, and going through Saturday, May 20th, the organization in North Texas will be hosting its Annual Hall of Fame induction ceremony. The event will include museum tours, a comedy show, an outdoor wrestling event, a meet and greet, and the induction banquet. The entire event will take place over three days.

"It's a great weekend and there is going to be a lot of fun," Mantell stated. "Fans will be able to see nearly 60 wrestlers over the entire weekend."

The main reason for the celebration is to honor the men and women who have dedicated years of their lives to a profession that has entertained millions of people for over a entury. Wrestlers like Stan Hansen, Terry Funk, Gene Kiniski,

Bruiser Brody, Orville Brown, and Dick Beyer, are some past inductees that will be met by an incredibly deserving new class of wrestlers.

"I think the stories from all of these guys in the past need to be told," Mantell explained. "If we don't recognize the people who came before us, the only people being recognized will be WWE people. I think that is a travesty for the sport to recognize only one group."

This year's organization will have 11 inductees. Yvonne Robert and "Dirty Dick" Raines are representing the Pioneer Category. Luther Lindsay and Sputnik Monroe will represent the Television Era. Shawn Michaels and Mick Foley will be honored for the Modern Era. Susan "Tex" Green and George Napolitano are acknowledged in the Ladies and Colleague Category. Larry Hennig and Harley Race will represent the Tag-Team and Tatsumi Fujinami will be honored in the International Division.

"There is not an unworthy person on this list that is going in the Hall of Fame this year," Mantell declared. "We are proud of this class and we are excited that five of the inductees plan to come to Wichita Falls for the ceremony."

When you look at the selection for the Ladies Category, the PWHF committee got it right. Susan "Tex" Green had a ton of wrestling talent, but if she did not, she could get into the Hall of Fame on her passion for the sport alone. Green grew up as a fan going to wrestling shows with her Father. After years of asking promoter Joe Blanchard to help her get into the sport, he finally did, and by the time she was 15, Green had her first professional match in 1969. Green had a long and successful wrestling career and now that she has put up her boots, she is still training and working out with people in the ring these days.

"She beat Moolah one night for the NWA World Title, and the NWA wouldn't recognize it because that wasn't supposed to happen," Mantell affirmed. "Just telling you that, should tell you everything you need to know about Susan 'Tex' Green."

Coming all the way over from Japan will be Tatsumi Fujinami. The wrestler from the land of the rising sun has held many titles in his long career, which dates back to 1971. Being the NWA World Heavyweight Champion and holding IWGP Heavyweight Championship six different times might settle any argument about his greatness. Fujinami had spent most of his career wrestling with New Japan Pro Wrestling, and because Mantell has had the opportunity to wrestle in Japan himself, he is very familiar with Fujinami's in-the-ring talent.

"I was so fortunate to get to wrestle with him and it always felt like a competition," Mantell recalled. "I have always enjoyed that feeling of working hard in the ring."

Some might be unaware that Larry Hennig and Harley Race were ever a tag team, but I assure you that their union was solid and the accomplishments they had together were credible. The two men crossed paths in their careers during the mid-1960s and shortly thereafter, captured the AWA World Tag Team Championship by defeating Dick the Bruiser and The Crusher. While Hennig and Race wrestled together, they held the prestigious belts on two other occasions.

"Those two were quite the tag team and they stopped working together because Harley went to the NWA and became the World Champion," Mantell said. "They wrestled the very best, and they were very talented wrestlers."

Those are just a few of the legends that will be honored at the Pro Wrestling Hall of Fame this year. On Friday night, the Pro Wrestling Hall of Fame will put on a wrestling event that will take place in a ring in downtown Wichita Falls on 8th and Ohio Street. Some of the wrestlers in action that night will be Andrew Anderson, Tyson Dean, Tokyo Monster Kahagas, Barrett Brown, and several others.

"It's a celebration of wrestling," Mantell attested. "All of these wrestlers come to Wichita Falls to let the fans know that wrestling is still alive."

ALVIN MINNICK – APRIL 28, 2017

Photo Courtesy of Alvin Minnick

When famous names in wrestling come up in a conversation, you may mention Ric Flair, Bruno Sammartino, Harley Race, and Terry Funk. The name Alvin Minnick might not come up in that same conversation, but he too has a place in professional wrestling. The man who grew up watching Memphis wrestling has been a wrestler, a manager, and a booker. Alvin might not have left the same impression that Jerry Lawler and Bill Dundee did when they were on television, but he has been in and around wrestling for over 30 years. Currently, he is booking with Greg Anthony in the NWA Mid South promotion.

"I have loved wrestling from the time I was growing up until now. Every aspect of it" Minnick answered. "When you walk out into that crowd and hear the yelling and the booing, it's a rush."

Minnick started wrestling in 1983 with his childhood friend Doug Worley, and they wrestled at outlaw shows in Dyersburg, Tennessee, and Malden, Missouri. Minnick took a break from wrestling between 1984 and 1987 when he served in the U.S. Army. When he returned home, he was back trying to get his big break in wrestling.

"The outlaw shows are what you would call the independent shows now," Minnick confirmed. "The bigger promotions looked down on us, but we were just starting out and couldn't make it on T.V. yet."

Alvin wrestled under the name of Mr. Charisma, and in 1991, he found the opportunity he was looking for. He started wrestling for the USWA, a promotion run by Jerry Jarrett, Buddy Wayne, and Eddie Marlin. While working there he used the name Al Hodge and he wrestled guys such as Brian Christopher, Doug Gilbert, King Cobra, and Dutch Mantell.

"At that time, the USWA was the biggest thing going. It was a dream come true for me," Minnick added. "I was in the same dressing room as Lawler, Valiant, Steve Keirn, and the Gilberts."

It finally had looked as if all the hard work that Minnick had invested into his wrestling career started to pay off. Unfortunately, he suffered an injury that forced him to stop wrestling altogether. The injury was so serious that his chiropractor thought that he should see a neurosurgeon. Alvin did not want anything to do with surgery. So, his chiropractor tried some different methods of treatment and they started to see some progress. That was almost 25 years ago and though he never had surgery, he continues to get chiropractic treatment.

"When you can't do something you love to do, and you are watching people you know who are doing it, it brings you way down," Minnick sighed. I had tears in my eyes because I knew I couldn't go back out there and wrestle."

When Minnick was able to get back on his feet he stayed close to the business. He started managing wrestlers, and from time to time he got involved in the action. In 1994, he had his first crack at booking matches in Dyersburg with All American Championship Wrestling. For the next couple of years, he was in and out of the business. In 1997, he got a call to book for the Warrior of Wrestling Federation, which eventually turned into the NWA Mid South.

"We drew in some crowds. It was a time when wrestling was hot," Minnick boasted. "When I could put something together that kept the crowd coming back, that was satisfying to me."

It was so satisfying for Alvin that he wanted to keep the momentum going. He often sat in the crowd and watched the fans cheer. He also observed their reaction and he could tell what they liked and what he needed to work on as a booker. Alvin did not make a lot of money in wrestling, but he has gained a wealth of knowledge and a strong understanding of what it takes to be successful in the sport.

"I get a rush from it when the crowd is into it from the start to the finish," Minnick stated. "I tell the guys all the time that the opening match sets the tone for the entire night."

In 2012, Minnick started promoting when Greg Anthony was hired to be the booker. Together the two have been successfully putting on over 100 shows a year. NWA Mid South has a wrestling event in Ripley, Tennessee every Friday night and one in Dyersburg, Tennessee every Saturday night.

"We put on a good professional show and they are family-oriented," Minnick replied. "There are fans out there that want to see good wrestling and I feel like we do that for them."

Photo Courtesy of Alvin Minnick

Alvin Minnick in 2019

PWHF 2017 TAG TEAM INDUCTEES – MAY 3, 2017

Photo by Melissa Woodruff   Photo Courtesy of Harley Race

Larry Hennig   **Harley Race**

When it comes to the Pro Wrestling Hall of Fame and Museum in Wichita Falls, Texas, their main goal is to preserve wrestling history. This year, the tag team being honored at their induction ceremony on May 18th through May 20th, will be Larry "The Ax" Hennig and Harley Race.

"We made a great team because we didn't do any of the same things," Larry Hennig recalled. "He was a specialist in some areas and I was a specialist in other areas."

Hennig was a little bigger than Harley and he was very strong. Being a Minnesota State Wrestling Champion in high school, Larry's amateur background showed up in his pro career on the mat. Race had the speed, endurance and he liked using the ropes. He did not mind taking a bump when he had to.

"He did every part of the wrestling that I didn't care to do and I did the parts that I liked to do, and that's how it went," Race responded. "You had to be fairly tough and we could both handle just about anything."

When the two wrestlers met in the early 1960s, Larry weighed nearly 340 pounds and Harley weighed around 280. Their wrestling styles complimented each other while they were competing against other teams in the ring. Their wrestling styles were not the only thing that made them successful.

"We had good attitudes, we worked hard, and we showed up to all of our events," Hennig confirmed. "We were a good combination. There wasn't anybody better than us."

The two captured their first AWA World Tag Team
Championship together on January 30th, 1965, when they
defeated Dick the Bruiser and the Crusher in Minneapolis,
Minnesota. The two teams battled each other on countless
occasions over the next couple of years throughout the Midwest.

"They were two of toughest guys at that point in time,"
Race remembered. "When you put yourself in the ring with those
two guys you were in a hell of a mix."

Race and Hennig dominated the Tag Team Division, not
only in the Midwest but all over the world. The two also traveled
together to wrestle in countries such as Japan and Australia. Their
skills and abilities in the ring proved them to be successful there
as well. The two men were a match made in heaven. Not just in
the ring, but also in life.

"I don't think I can ever remember the two of us ever
having an argument," Race recalled. "We liked each other."

Back then, when wrestlers worked together it was easy to
be around someone for days and even weeks at a time. Traveling
in a car or on plane with someone you did not get along with
made for a long trip. Whether it was an understanding or just
mutual respect, the two wrestlers were loyal friends.

"I liked the guy and he liked me," said Hennig. "When
Harley told you something he kept his word."

They held the AWA World Tag Team titles together a total
of three times. Unfortunately in 1967, Larry suffered a serious
injury to his knee during a match. He returned to ring action a
year later and worked alongside his friend and tag partner. Later
that year, Harley left the AWA and went to the NWA to pursue a
singles career. On May 24th, 1973, Race defeated Dory Funk Jr. to
become the NWA World's Heavyweight Champion. That
particular win was the first of his eight title reigns with the
wrestling promotion throughout his lengthy career. On that
special night, Race did not have his former tag team partner in his
corner, but Larry was in the crowd.

"I was there and I was very proud of him," Hennig
grinned. "He was the man. He had it all, he was the full package."

Both wrestlers went their different directions, but ironically, both of their careers lasted for about 30 years. They have maintained their friendship since they first met. They wrestled together, they made money together, they traveled together, and now they are going into the Pro Wrestling Hall of Fame together.

"Me and Larry were a great tag team," Race informed. "Being honored with him is great for me and for wrestling too."

LARRY HENNIG
June 18, 1936 – December 6, 2018

HARLEY RACE
April 11, 1943 – August 1, 2019

BARRETT BROWN – MAY 8, 2017

Jon-Paul Le Blanc - 4 Corners Photography

Not too many wrestlers at the age of 23 can say they have been wrestling for eight years. Not unless that wrestler started when they were 15 years old. For Barrett Brown from Seven Points, Texas, he did. His mother had always known of his passion for the sport, so she got in touch with one of her friends that did some professional wrestling around the North Texas area. His name was Cody Cunningham and he agreed to train the determined teenager.

"Wrestling was always a part of my family and I just grew up with it," Barrett Brown stated. "I always wanted to know what it felt like to be in front of a crowd and to be a larger-than-life figure for the fans. So that was always an aspiration for me."

Barrett met with Cunningham and they became really good friends. The two trained off and on together for about four years. Cunningham was able to pass on a solid foundation of basic wrestling skills to the young teen.

"He taught me the bare basics of wrestling. I had no idea of what I was getting into," Brown admitted. "Despite my age, he treated me like an adult and he didn't hold anything back."

Before he was 16 years old, Barrett had his very first match at a small local show near Dallas. After Brown had been wrestling for a year, he wanted to grow as a wrestler. So, he reached out to Killer Tim Brooks and Johnny Mantell. They were both veteran wrestlers that had successful careers in the business.

"I wanted to branch out further than just the small local shows. So, I went to train with them," Brown explained. "I got on some of their shows and they opened a lot of doors for me even though I was so young."

Brooks and Mantell stressed the fundamentals of wrestling and the importance of paying attention to the details. He was taught psychology, history, and how to appreciate the business. One of Barrett's big breaks in his career came when he was just 18 years old. That was when he started wrestling on television under Matt Riviera's promotion called Traditional Championship Wrestling based in Arkansas.

"People that I had worked with were telling me if I ever had a chance to get on that roster to do it," Brown commented. "That was when I felt like I was getting the ball rolling."

With Brown being on the Traditional Championship roster, it proved to be an important step in his career. Not only was he getting his name out in public with the T.V. exposure, but he was also given opportunities to wrestle some famous names in the sport. Barrett got to wrestle a true legend in Cowboy Bob Orton. Orton is a second-generation wrestler and the Father of WWE superstar Randy Orton. He started wrestling in 1972 and has wrestled all over the United States and around the world. The Cowboy has been associated with a countless number of promotions including the NWA, WWE, and All Japan Pro Wrestling. During his career, he has held many championship titles.

"I think that was the biggest match that I have had in my career, name-wise. I got two years of knowledge just by being in the ring with him one night," Brown joked. "He has been wrestling longer than I have been alive. I didn't know what good wrestling was until I got in the ring with him."

Brown pinned Orton which was a huge win for him, but what he gained by being in the ring with the veteran wrestler was priceless. After wrestling with Orton, Brown noticed that his footwork and timing started to improve when he was working with his other opponents.

"He helped with those two things and that is what I took from him after having that match," Brown recalled. "I was able to learn a lot of knowledge that I was able to incorporate with what I already knew to get better."

Now that Barrett has been traveling he has been introduced to different wrestling styles. The confidence he now has in his in-ring abilities is growing. He wants to win the NWA Jr. Heavyweight Championship that is currently held by Arrick Andrews. In 2012, Brown had a shot at wrestling for that title when Kevin Douglas was the Champion. However, after 15 minutes, the match was stopped by the referee due to interference. Even though things did not end the way he had hoped for, it was still a special moment for Barrett in his career.

"It was very surreal to me because I wasn't even 19 at the time. I didn't expect to receive anything that important until I was 20," Brown said. "I think we put on such a good match because our styles were so similar. It was like a clashing of the minds."

While growing up as a wrestling fan, Barrett knew that the NWA World Heavyweight Championship was the title of all titles. At five feet six inches and 160 pounds, the junior title is a closer reality for Brown to achieve. Putting that belt around his waist meant more to him than just being Champion.

"My original trainer Cody was a big NWA fan," Brown recalled. "If I win that title, I'd be able to show him that I did it. It would make everything that we have worked for worth it."

Jon-Paul Le Blanc - 4 Corners Photography
D-Lo Brown vs. Barrett Brown - May 19, 2018

VAN VAN HORNE - MAY 13, 2017

Photo Courtesy of Van Van Horne

54-year-old Van Van Horne is from Memphis, Tennessee. He started wrestling when he was 22. In three decades, he has wrestled professionally for only five years. Some might have certain perceptions about his short career, but for Van Horne it has been pretty amazing.

"I tell everybody that I am the Forest Gump of professional wrestling. I'm nobody, but I've been in the right place to be able to do some really cool stuff," Van Van Horne said. "I had wrestled for all three major promotions at one time, and I wrestled some amazing guys in the sport."

Van Horne has experienced it all. He was just like anybody else when he started in wrestling. He just wanted his big break. Van Horne thought he got that chance while wrestling in Memphis under Jerry Jarrett's Championship Wrestling promotion. At the time, Jerry Lawler was the booker. It was there Van wrestled in a tag team with John Stewart called The Beach Boys and they wore sunglasses and Jamz, which are colorful cotton, knee-high shorts.

Although Van Horne was newly married, because he believed the promoter was finally giving him and his partner the push they were looking for, he quit his full-time job. Stewart was about 230 pounds and he had a stocky build, so his body did not adapt well to the restricted material that the Jamz had to offer. The shorts ripped on him during their matches often. One day after a match John asked Jerry Lawler if he could wear spandex instead.

Five minutes passed and the Beach Boys received a visit from him.

"Jerry says John, I thought about what you said, and how about I just fire you tonight? Our chins hit the ground," Van Horne recalled. "Jerry wasn't going to let anybody who only had five matches tell him anything about the wrestling business."

Not only did Stewart get fired, but so did Van Horne and their push ended that night. Van Horne returned to working a full-time job, but at the same time, he was reaching out to his contacts on the independent wrestling scene. Before long, he found a new tag team partner in Motley Cruz. The two men dressed up as baseball players and took up the name, River City Bombers. They begin to make a name for themselves and started wrestling every weekend throughout the South Eastern region of the United States. While in Missouri, they got booked by Bill Ash and they wrestled on some cards with Bruiser Brody.

Bruiser Brody loved their baseball gimmick and in the early part of 1987, he booked the River City Bombers on some shows in St. Louis. Right away they were in matches with Bobby Fulton and Tommy Rogers, the Fantastics. After a few shows with Brody, he told Cruz and Van Horne that he wanted to take them to Japan for a tour. In Japan, both baseball and wrestling are very popular and Brody thought the River City Bombers would be a hit over there.

"In our last conversation we had with Brody, he told us to get our passports ready," Van Horne added. "We didn't get to see him again and the next thing we heard was that he was killed in Puerto Rico."

Shortly after Brody's death, a fellow wrestler named Larry Williams told Van Horne that he was going to the WWF. He mentioned that they were looking for new guys to work with their superstars. At that time, the WWF was going strong and the Steamboat–Savage era was about to take off. Van Horne jumped at the offer. Before long he was wrestling against guys such as Bret Hart, Rick Rude, Greg Valentine, and Randy Savage. Van was a "jobber" and his main purpose was to make the top talent there look good.

"I couldn't believe who I was working with on the biggest stage in professional wrestling," Van Horne beamed. "I was glad to be there, I didn't care what my role was."

Over a six month period, Van wrestled in 14 matches with the WWF. If he was not getting beat up by the One Man Gang or Bam Bam Bigelow in single matches, he and a partner were losing to teams like the British Bulldogs, the Hart Foundation, and Demolition. Eventually, Van Horne got a full-time job with Federal Express and was not able to travel during the week anymore. That led to the end of his wrestling career in the WWF. Participating in a few matches here and there, life started to change for Van Horne. He started to experience some opportunities and more responsibilities with his full-time job.

"It was disappointing because I made some good connections with some other job guys. I ended up going out to Las Vegas to the Showboat twice and I did some shows for the AWA." Van explained. "At that time, Vince McMahon was pulling in all the great talent from everywhere and the AWA started to suffer."

In 2003, Van moved back to Memphis, and after a few months of being home, he called up his former tag team partner Motley Cruz. Van found out where his friend was training in Dyersburg, and he went to check it out. After Van's daughter was born in 2004, he tried wrestling once again, but his heart just was not into it. Now 52 years old, Van Horne started thinking it was time to get back into the gym to see if he could put on a little muscle. After a few months of working out and seeing some changes in his body, he considered calling Greg Anthony, a wrestler he met in Dyersburg 10 years earlier.

"I had no idea he was a part of the NWA promotion and what he had done with his career," Van Horne continued. "I told him I was thinking about wrestling again, but I needed someone I could trust to run me through the motions. I didn't know if I could do it at my age."

A week later, he found himself driving to Dyersburg to meet up with Greg. The two men briefly talked about how they were going to approach the day's training schedule. Van got into the ring with one of Greg's trainees, and after a couple of moves, Van took a shoulder tackle and hit the mat. It was as if he had never been away from the sport and his passion for wrestling was back.

Today, Van Horne is wrestling in the NWA Mid-South Promotion. He and his partner Drop Dead Dale Wylde wrestle under the name The Love Connection, and they currently hold the NWA Mid South Tag Team Championship.

In November, Van Horne got to fulfill his lifelong dream. He stepped in the ring for his very first NWA Heavyweight Title match against Champion Tim Storm. To Van Horne, it was a big deal, because many wrestlers in the business never get that chance. It was an opportunity that he did not expect, but one he is grateful for. The match only lasted about 20 minutes, with Storm winning by a pin fall. Though he came up short, it was an experience Van Horne will never forget.

"A lot of people discount the NWA because it is not what it used to be, but at last count, the NWA was at 32 promotions," Van Horne said. "If you are in the ring competing for a belt that represents 32 different companies, that is still a pretty big deal to me."

When Van Horne looks back over his wrestling career, it humbles him. He has a hard time wrapping his mind around who he has been in the ring with. Besides being 54, Van still feels that he is young when it comes to his in-ring wrestling ability. Last summer, he did a wrestling camp with Harley Race, and while he was there he met Hiroshi Tanahashi, an accomplished Japanese wrestler. Meeting Tanahashi brought back memories from years ago that Van Horne has never forgotten.

"I still want to go and wrestle in Japan. I want to go fulfill that opportunity I had with Brody before he died," Van Horne confirmed. "That has always eaten at me all of these years and I still feel like I can physically do it."

ARRICK ANDREWS – MAY 18, 2017

Jon-Paul Le Blanc - 4 Corners Photography

Professional wrestling has a rich history. That history is intertwined with colorful characters and prestigious titles. The fans who follow the sport understand that tradition and it is carried on by wrestling's champions. Angelo Savoldi, Danny Hodge, Nelson Royal, and Chase Owens will forever be listed in the wrestling books as the NWA Jr. Heavyweight Titleholders. Arrick Andrews of Gallatin, Tennessee is also in that same group.

"It is an honor and a privilege to be wrestling in the longest-running promotion. Even though it isn't as strong as it once was, the history and the tradition is something you can't replace," Arrick Andrews explained. "To me, there is nothing comparable to being the World Jr. Heavyweight Champion for the NWA. The NWA is respected by every professional wrestler."

The 33-year-old wrestler has been lacing up his boots for the last 16 years. In that time he has experienced some special moments, but nothing compares to the accomplishment that took place on April 8th of this year. On that day, he defeated the formidable John Saxon in their match in Dyersburg. Saxon who had been champion for almost a full year met his match in Andrews.

"John is a true professional on every level. He knows wrestling inside and out," Andrews said. "If you show him a weakness, he is going to exploit it. From the beginning of the match until the very end, John brought everything he had."

Andrews and Saxon met in the ring initially the night before he captured the title. The fans in Tullahoma, Tennessee were excited to witness an NWA Jr. Title defense.

However, the spectators supporting Andrews were disappointed when Saxon was awarded the win. Moments after the match, officials had determined that the Champion had cheated, and the NWA made an announcement to the crowd. "I thought I was going to become Champion that night, but I got screwed out of it," Andrews continued. "Afterwards, the NWA came out and scheduled a rematch for the next night. It was a huge relief for me."

In their second meeting, the match lasted approximately 30 minutes. The two wrestlers battled in a grueling contest that went back and forth throughout the entire contest. Saxon and Andrews kept the crowd guessing as each man regained the upper hand. Finally, Andrews caught the Champion with a Spine Buster and he was able to get the victory and win the title.

"It was hard to find his weakness and to catch him off guard. He was on cue every step of the way," Andrews affirmed. "It was one of those things that when it happened, I wanted to cry because I was finally a world champion."

Now that Andrews is on top, he knows that the bar has been raised. He believes he has a certain responsibility to carry the title of NWA Jr. Heavyweight Champion with high standards and character. If Arrick thinks that there is pressure outside of the ring now that he is Champion, he will feel it when he is inside the ring as well. Since holding the belt, Andrews has defended it in five different states and has put it on the line several times in one week.

"As far as the competition goes, guys are coming out of the woodwork for a title shot," Andrews pointed out. "I tell people all the time, get a match booked I will be there."

Every promotion has a hungry wrestler who thinks he deserves a title shot against Andrews. Being the World's Champion means that you fight the best that wrestling has to offer. Right now, some of the guys that are waiting in line to take their chances at Andrews are Jeremy Moore, Americos, and Mr. USA.

"I have wrestled Mr. USA a couple of times since winning the title and there is no doubt he is a solid challenge," Andrews stated. "As for him being the next NWA Jr. Heavyweight Champion, I don't see it happening. He has already had some chances and he hasn't been able to get the job done."

Many wrestlers get into the business with aspirations of being the World Champion. For now, Andrews can scratch that goal off his list. His main focus is to continue to stay strong and healthy so he can remain on top for a long time to come. After wrestling in every region of the United States, he now wants to wrestle overseas.

"I want to go to places like Japan, England, and Australia. Their fan bases are completely different," Andrews remarked. "What the fans like over there is unlike the United States. I have always prided myself in being able to adapt."

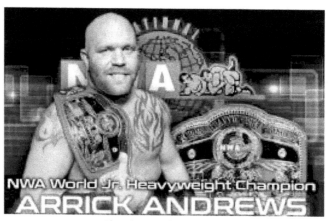

Photo Courtesy of James Carver

Arrick Andrews in 2017

MR. USA – MAY 22, 2017

Photo Courtesy of James Carver

Professional wrestler Mr. USA has been in the sport for the past eight years. On May 19th, he won the NWA Jr. Heavyweight Title when he defeated Arrick Andrews by pin fall in their match in Franklin, Kentucky. Wrestleville had a chance to talk to Mr. USA about his big win, his opponent, and what he expects for his career in the near future.

Q: What does it mean for you to be the new NWA World Jr. Heavyweight Champion?

A: It means the world to me as far as the wrestling business is concerned. Everybody who ever laced up a pair of boots dreams of being a World's Champion and that dream was achieved Friday night for me. I had asked the referee if that was a three count and he then handed me the belt. At that moment it became very real.

Q: After the match, you were met by some of your fellow wrestlers in the ring. Who all came out to support you and what did that mean to you?

A: It brought tears to my eyes because I love every one of those guys that came out to meet me in the ring. Former National Champion Damien Wayne came out to see me. Former NWA World Champion Rob Conway was there in addition to my trainer Chris Michaels. Those three names alone mean so much to pro wrestling and they all have done so much for this sport. They all have been former champions in some capacity across this great country. Promoter Tim Thomason and up-and-coming wrestler Sean Hurley were there as well. It meant a lot. My wife, kids, and mother were in attendance, so it was a very special moment for me and it was very surreal.

Q: What does it mean to you when you think about the wrestlers that have held that belt before you?

A: When you look at the history of this belt, it has been around for years. After the match, Rob Conway hugged me and said that my name was now in the record books. That is something that can't be taken away from me. My name cannot be erased.

Q: What kind of an opponent and what kind of champion was Arrick Andrews?

A: He is very tough. He trains in Jiu-Jitsu and other Mix Martial Arts, so Arrick is a very tough individual inside and outside of the ring. He is a great competitor and he has been around for a long time. He has done so much for the sport of wrestling that he has fans everywhere he goes. Even though he is somewhat of a bad guy, he still gets a lot of cheers from the crowd. I credit that to his in-ring ability and the respect he shows the fans. I think he is a great guy, but he just takes a lot of shortcuts nowadays.

Q: Is it true that if you did not defeat Arrick this time, that you would never get a shot at that belt again?

A: Yes sir. That was what I was told. If I didn't win on Friday night, I wouldn't get another shot at his belt.

Q: Who told you that?

A: I got a text message from Tim Thomason, the promoter of NWA New South and SAW Promotions. If I was unable to pin Arrick Andrews in that match, that was it. I wasn't told why. I can only speculate. I already had three chances to win the belt previously. I had to get the job done and I understood that.

Q: Do you think that Andrews will be receiving a rematch from you soon?

A: I will give him a rematch for sure. He didn't want to give me another shot at the belt, but the NWA made him. So I will give him his. I don't want to be one of these champions that doesn't defend his championship. I will defend my belt against anybody, anywhere. When it is time for Arrick to get his rematch, I will be there anytime and any place.

Q: Now that you are champion, do you expect there to be more pressure on you, and will the competition be tougher?

A: It feels like the pressure is already on. As a world champion, I wonder if I can live up to the expectations, am I good enough? Now that I here, am I going to be able to stay here? The competition is so brutal. Arrick has taken that title everywhere and I think about living up to those standards and wanting to take it further. It is a challenge that I welcome and I am excited to see what I can do with it.

Q: Do you feel by achieving this accomplishment you have secured a place for your name in wrestling history?

A: By winning the championship from Arrick Andrews, my name will be in the record books for good. I will also be recognized for taking the belt off of Arrick Andrews, he is no slouch. He has also held the NWA National Title.

Q: When it is all said and done, how do you want to be remembered, and what do you want your legacy in wrestling to be?

A: I'd like to be known as somebody that didn't take any crap. That I worked hard, and I fought anybody anywhere. I hope they remember me as being a fighting champion.

Q: Why do you wear a mask?

A: I have been a wrestling fan since I was a kid. I have always wanted to be a wrestler. The very first time I wrestled, I didn't wear a mask and I was scared to death. I had no personality at all. Someone suggested that I try wearing a mask. As a result, I was able to create a different personality because people didn't know it's me underneath the hood. I tried it and the fans seemed to love it. It's not very common to see a masked wrestler on the independent scene anymore.

FUN FACTS
Favorite wrestler: Ric Flair.
Career Highlight: Wrestled Jerry Lawler.
Favorite bands: Sawyer Brown and Ac-Dc.
Favorite sports team: Chicago Cubs.
Hobbies: Fishing, boating, and shooting guns.
Dog person or cat person: Neither .
State you have never been to: California.

Photo Courtesy of James Carver

Arrick Andrews vs. Mr. USA - May 19, 2017

BOBBY FULTON – MAY 29, 2017

Picture Courtesy of Bobby Fulton

Bobby Fulton & Tommy Rogers

In the Southern region of the United States back in the 80s, there were a slew of tag teams that dominated their opponents inside the squared circle. They were The Sheepherders, The Rock n Roll Express, The Midnight Express, and The Fabulous Ones. When it came to Bobby Fulton and Tommy Rogers, they were known as the Fantastics and fantastic they were.

"It was like magic. We worked hard and we just clicked as a team," Bobby Fulton remarked. "It was just like a marriage. The two of us excelled in certain areas, but we filled in the gaps for each other when we needed to."

It was known throughout the locker room that the Fantastics had a good work ethic. Fellow wrestler Arn Anderson joked with Bobby and Tommy about not wanting to be in the match after they had wrestled, because it was always a hard act to follow. There were times the Fantastics got upset with their opponent's performance because they did not always meet their expectations.

"Sometimes guys were tired and they layed down. They wouldn't want to do anything," Fulton recalled. "One night, we were walking to the dressing room and promoter Jim Barnett approached us. He said if we always worked hard in the ring we would never have a bad match. Jim gave each of us an extra thousand dollars that night on top of our payout."

Bobby and Tommy met in Memphis, Tennessee in 1983. They were later brought together to be wrestling partners by Bill Dundee. At the time Bill was a booker for Bill Watt's Mid-South Promotion. The Fantastics' role was to be a 90-day replacement team for the Rock n' Roll Express in Louisiana. Rogers and Fulton remained friends for the next 30 years up until Rogers' untimely death in 2015. He was only 54 years old.

The day Fulton received the news about Tommy's death might have been one of the worst days of his life. Even though he misses Tommy and thinks of him often, Fulton is filled with so many fond memories of his late tag team partner. In the 30 years that the Fantastics were friends, brothers, and wrestling partners, they shared some incredible moments. Some might compare their lives to those of rock stars.

"It hurt. We were family and he was my brother," Fulton sighed. "He was a man that helped me realize my dreams in professional wrestling. We were a well-oiled team."

Whether it was Memphis, Mid-South, World Class, UWF, or the Mid-Atlantic territories, the Fantastics held titles together everywhere they wrestled. The most prestigious belts they have held throughout their career were the NWA United States Tag Team Titles on two different occasions. If the pair defended their titles or chased after them, their popularity soared. As soon as their entrance music was heard, the fans, the majority of them being women, flocked to ringside so they could get close to them.

"I wanted to be a wrestler as long as I could remember," Fulton said. "I was glad that the fans wanted to hug me and they accepted us, but we were always rushing to the next town. We couldn't stop and smell the roses."

Having the attention of adoring women might have been flattering for two young men in their 20s, but oftentimes, it was overwhelming. The lines of reality and fantasy were often blurred and sometimes it even caused them a problem or two.

"We were both married at the time. Even when we were out with our wives, we were mobbed by so many women that they knocked our wives down to the ground," Fulton mentioned. "I looked over and my wife would be pushed out of the way and upset. A married woman doesn't like that obviously."

Leaving the venues was also a challenge. On many occasions the two wrestlers sped while driving to get home or going to the next event. Sometimes it became exhausting and a bit strange for the Fantastic wrestling team.

"We couldn't go to our homes because the women followed us everywhere we went. If we drove 100 miles per hour, they drove 105," Fulton said. "When we opened our doors to our homes or hotel rooms, there was pizza, food, and jewelry all stacked up outside. It was unbelievable!"

When Fulton and Rogers weren't being consumed by their fans leaving the venues, they were being attacked by their opponents during their matches. They had some epic battles in the ring, many of those were with The Midnight Express. Some of the most grueling and bloodiest matches that they had were against the Sheepherders during their time in the UWF in 1986.

"We had something like 37 barbed wire cage matches in a row with them. It was just blood and guts," Fulton cringed. "The promoters had us there for the women, but when we were in there with the Sheepherders the blood was flying. The guys in the crowd could see that we could fight too."

If going toe to toe with Butch Miller and Luke Williams did not say that the Fantastics were tough, maybe wrestling with a torn rotator cuff and a broken neck does. While the two worked in Dallas for Fritz Von Erich, Bobby wrestled in nearly 40 matches in three weeks knowing his shoulder was seriously injured. When they were on tour in Japan Tommy went to warm up in the ring before the matches started. He attempted to dive the top rope, but landed wrong on the mat and broke his neck. Tommy was hurt, but he did not realize the severity of the injury and went ahead and wrestled that night anyway.

"Back then, you had to do that if you wanted to stay in professional wrestling. No one wanted to lose their spot," Fulton claimed. "Tommy was tough. He would have fought a buzz saw. He even fought David Shultz."

By the end of the 90s, the team of Fulton and Rogers came to an end. Bobby had children and Tommy was slowed down by his injuries. Eventually, both men lived on opposite sides of the country from each other. Though they did not participate in each other's lives like they had done in the past on a daily basis, they were still very close. In the last year of Tommy's life, the two friends spent a lot of time talking about the Bible, their salvation, and Jesus Christ. Both men experienced a sense of peace in theirself when they accepted Jesus as their Lord and Savior.

"He was searching and seeking and he was reading the scriptures," Fulton replied. "It brought me comfort as a believer to see him doing that."

The initial pain from the news of Tommy's death has subsided, but that feeling of loss will probably never go away. The memories of Tommy are still alive in Bobby's mind. The Fantastics were like brothers and they shared a lot of life. Even though they both were not huge wrestlers as far as their body size, they accomplished a lot in the sport that the bigger guys were never able to achieve.

TOMMY ROGERS
May 14, 1961 – June 1, 2015

JOSH LEWIS – JUNE 7, 2017

Picture Courtesy of Josh Lewis

Bodybuilder turned wrestler, Josh Lewis has only been wrestling professionally since 2015. In that short time, he has accomplished so much. On May 27th, Lewis defeated Rob Conway in Madison, Indiana to regain the NWA United States Championship, a title he lost to Conway just 15 days prior. This is the third time Lewis has held the belt and he is currently ranked number nine in the NWA rankings. I had a chance to talk to Lewis the day after his big win.

Q: What does it mean to you to be the NWA United States Champion?

A: It means absolutely everything to me to have this title. To me, any title in the National Wrestling Alliance is huge. Even though it might not be the same U.S. title that Dusty Rhodes and Lex Lugar held, it is still a version of it and it's important to me.

Q: What kind of an opponent was Rob Conway in your rematch?

A: Rob is one of the best wrestlers in the business. He is a former NWA World Champion and a former WWE Tag Team Champion. He has even wrestled in Japan. He has done just everything there is to do in wrestling and he has been very successful. To win the title is special, but to win it from the Ironman Rob Conway is huge.

Q: Does that add to your confidence that you have beaten a two-time NWA World Heavyweight Champion?

A: Absolutely. Rob is such a famous person in pro wrestling, and his name alone can draw so many people to an event. To win the title from him is a highlight for my career so far.

Q: What do you hope this victory says about you and where you are in your career?

A: I hope the promoters and my fellow wrestlers see that I am here to stay. I want to be known as an NWA guy, especially with all the news and excitement about the company recently being sold. I'm sure that by Billy Corgan buying the NWA, he plans to do something with it and hopefully one day we can get back on T.V. There is so much prestige with someone being an NWA champion. I was so excited last night and my adrenaline was pumping so fast I could hardly go to sleep.

Q: Do you think this win says that you are ready for a shot at the NWA National, the North American, or even the World title?

A: Yes. I have had a couple of shots against Greg Anthony for the National Title, but I came up short. With me moving along in my wrestling career, I feel like I am getting better and better with my skills since those opportunities. Hopefully, this win will put me in line for another shot down the road for one of those big titles.

Q: What is next for you in your career?

A: I want to continue to progress in the NWA and I am sure I will be having some rematches against Rob for the title. Hopefully, those go well. I plan to take it one match at a time.

Q: By holding this championship, do you expect the competition to get tougher?

A: As far as Rob Conway goes, I feel like I am working against one of the best guys out there. As my career continues, I hope to have a shot at the NWA World title. That title is the same prestigious belt that Ric Flair, Harley Race, Gene Kiniski, and Lou Thesz have held.

Q: How do you think your bodybuilding career has prepared you for wrestling?

A: I think it has made me very marketable. When I come from the curtain, the fans might not know who I am. But they see me as a star because I look like a star. A lot of guys in the sport today don't look the part anymore. As a young child, I wanted to look like Lex Lugar, Sting, and The Ultimate Warrior. I have a similar look to those guys now and I can say that my bodybuilding career has made me physically stronger than 99 percent of the guys out there. If you are not familiar with Josh Lewis, who does look marketable, you're thinking this guy is somebody.

Q: How and why do you think your bodybuilding career has given you a strong advantage?

A: I'm a 500-pound bench presser and I spent years and years developing my body and being on my diet. Working at being the best at competitions has helped me gain a certain look and it has helped me with my overall confidence. Not just in wrestling, but at everything I do in life.

Q: When your career is over what would you like your legacy in wrestling to be?

A: I would like to be the NWA World Champion one day. You never know if that will happen, but I am an individual who sets my goals high. That is the the ultimate goal for me.

Photo Courtesy of Josh Lewis

Josh Lewis - Cincinnati, Ohio - 2nd Place - 2011

ROB CONWAY

NWA WORLD HEAVYWEIGHT CHAMPION

1ST: March 16, 2013 - January 4, 2014
2ND: June 2, 2014 - February 14, 2015

NWA - BROWNSVILLE, TX
OCTOBER 18, 2011

Wrestleville – Vinny Berry

Adam Pearce

Big Dawg

Manimal

Chaz Taylor

Kevin Douglas

Rudy Russo

Dave Silva & Greg Valentine

NWA - BROWNSVILLE, TX
FEBRUARY 26, 2012

Wrestleville – Vinny Berry

Rudy Russo vs. Kevin Douglas

Hamebone Lee & Chaz Taylor

The Lumberjack vs. Lance Archer

Mike Dell

Houston Carson

Barbie Hayden

WILDKAT – METAIRIE, LA
MARCH 15, 2013
Jon-Paul Le Blanc - 4 Corners Photography

Rudy Russo vs. Haniel-T

Houston Carson, Bolt Brady, & BuKu Dao

Jack Jameson

Outlaw Matt Lancie vs. Carlos Soccoro

Luke Hawx

Steve Anthony vs. Wes Adams

OLDSKOOL – WESTWEGO, LA
SEPTEMBER 21, 2013

Jon-Paul Le Blanc - 4 Corners Photography

Mustang Mike vs. Marty Graw

T-Wolfe

Trucker Jones vs. Kegger

Trucker Jones & Xtian Blake

Hollywood Chuck vs. Mudd Dog

Rodney Mack vs. Minotaur

NWA NEW JAPAN INVASION – HOUSTON, TX
OCTOBER 18, 2013
Jon-Paul Le Blanc - 4 Corners Photography

Rob Conway

Jushin Thunder Liger

Davey Boy Smith Jr.

Jason Kincaid

Damien Wayne

Tenzan

Gedo vs. Hirori

Alex Reigns

James Claxton

WILDKAT - NEW ORLEANS, LA
NOVEMBER 15, 2013
Jon-Paul Le Blanc - 4 Corners Photography

Ricky Starks vs. Purple Haze

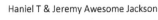

Haniel T & Jeremy Awesome Jackson

Luke Hawx

Mike Dell

Outlaw Matt Lancie vs. Stevie Richards

Minatour & Hard Body Harper

ELITE CHAMPIONSHIP WRESTLING – HOUMA, LA
JANUARY 26, 2014
Jon-Paul Le Blanc - 4 Corners Photography

Olympus, Scott Phoenix, & Purple Haze

Americos vs. Gary Roosevelt Gram

Tim Storm vs. Vordell Walker

Tim & Vordell in the crowd

Matt Rivera vs. Stan Sweetan

Sweetan escaping from a pin attempt

NWA SUMMER CLASH – BENTON, AR – JULY 4, 2014

Jon-Paul Le Blanc - 4 Corners Photography

Matt Riviera & Greg Anthony

Luke Williams greeting fans

Brian Thompson, Matt, Tim Stom,
& Greg Anthony

Bruce Tharpe, James Beard
& Bobby Eaton

Fermin Perez & Jax Dane

Mr. Saturday Night

NWA SUMMER CLASH – BENTON, AR – JULY 4, 2014

Jon-Paul Le Blanc - 4 Corners Photography

Luke Williams vs. Gary Roosevelt Gram

Mr. Saturday Night vs. Jax Dane

Jax Dane lifting John Saxon

Tim Storm vs. Ricky Morton

Ricky Morton vs. Greg Anthony

A.J. Styles

NWA MID ATLANTIC LEGENDS FEST – CHAROLETTE, NC
JULY 31, 2014
Jon-Paul Le Blanc - 4 Corners Photography

Bobby Fulton, Bill Mercer, & Jim Cornette

Ron Simmons, Rocky Johnson, & Vader

Magnum T. A. & Tully Blanchard

Larry Zbyszko

Tommy Young, Bob Caudle, & Les Thatcher

Justin Credible

NWA MID ATLANTIC LEGENDS FEST – CHAROLETTE, NC
JULY 31, 2014

Jon-Paul Le Blanc - 4 Corners Photography

Adrian Street & Miss Linda

Chase Owens, Robert Gibson, & Ricky Morton

Dave Millican

Scott Teal

Big Cat Ernie Miller

Kevin Sullivan, Nigel McGuiness, & J.J. Dillon

DAVID VON ERICH MEMORIAL – MESQUITE, TX
NOVEMBER 1, 2014

Jon-Paul Le Blanc - 4 Corners Photography

Manny Villalobos vs. Chaz Taylor

Angelina Sky

Kamala Jr. & Slam Shady

The Grappler & Slam Shady

The Grappler vs. Jamie Holley

Kevin Cross & Nigel Rabid

DAVID VON ERICH MEMORIAL – MESQUITE, TX
NOVEMBER 1, 2014

Jon-Paul Le Blanc - 4 Corners Photography

Christopher Daniel

Jason Silver

Marshall, Kevin, & Ross Von Erich

Eddie Edwards & Davey Richards

Kevin Von Erich putting the claw on Tim Brooks

Ken Johnson

NWA MAIN EVENT – PATTERSON, LA
DECEMBER 7, 2014

Jon-Paul Le Blanc - 4 Corners Photography

Buku Dao vs. Jo Jo Bravo

Machiko

Steve Anthony & Luke Hawx

Killer Shane Desmeroux

Danny Flamingo

Tim Storm vs. Haniel-T

NWA BOW - SAN ANTONIO, TX
FEBRUARY 21, 2015
Jon-Paul Le Blanc - 4 Corners Photography

Amber O'Neal vs. Barbie Hayden

Barbie Hayden & Luke Gallows

Houston Carson vs. Lance Hoyt

Keith Lee vs. Mike Dell

James Claxton & Ken Johnson

Rob Conway vs. James Claxton

GULF COAST WRESTLING REUNION – MOBILE, AL
MARCH 7, 2015

Jon-Paul Le Blanc - 4 Corners Photography

Ron Bass on the left & Gypsy Joe seated

Adrian Street, Ole Anderson, & Miss Linda

Elliot Wiggins

Don Fargo on the right

Ranger Ross

Mr.Olympia

LEGENDS FEST – DOTHAN, AL
MAY 9, 2015
Jon-Paul Le Blanc - 4 Corners Photography

Adrian Street & Col. Rob Parker

Ben Masters & Wendell Cooley

Robert Gibson

Ron Fuller

Ben Masters & Austin Idol

Chic Donavan & Big Ramp

BUSTIN 4 AUSTISM – PASADENA, TX
JULY 12, 2015
Jon-Paul Le Blanc - 4 Corners Photography

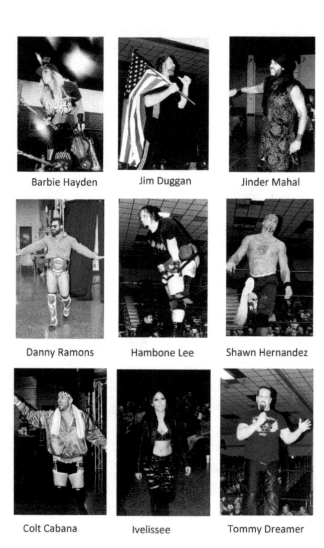

Barbie Hayden   Jim Duggan   Jinder Mahal

Danny Ramons   Hambone Lee   Shawn Hernandez

Colt Cabana   Ivelissee   Tommy Dreamer

COMBAT SPORTS PRO – PENSACOLA, FL
AUGUST 9, 2015

Jon-Paul Le Blanc - 4 Corners Photography

Suicydal Soldier diving onto Purple Haze

Purple Haze landing onto Suicydal Soldier

Ryan Oshun grabbing Vordell Walker

Steve Anthony vs. John Saxon

Ox Haney

Bob Armstrong, Teddy Long, & Lance Russell

WILDKAT – NEW ORLEANS, LA - AUGUST 15, 2015
Sabu vs. Danny Flamingo
Jon-Paul Le Blanc - 4 Corners Photography

Sabu getting help

Danny getting a chair

Sabu with a leg drop

Danny taking punishment

Melissa Coates

Sabu off the top rope

NWA – CROWLEY, TX
OCTOBER 31, 2015
Jon-Paul Le Blanc - 4 Corners Photography

Brandon Collins vs. John Allen

Gregory James

Moonshine Mantell vs. Ricky Starks

Americos vs. James Johnson

Americos diving

Referee James Beard

WRESTLECADE – WINSTON-SALEM, NC
NOVEMBER 28, 2015
Jon-Paul Le Blanc - 4 Corners Photography

Robert Gibson

Bobby Fulton

Sam Roberts

Jeff Hardy

John Hitchcock

Papa Stro

Bill Apter

The Patriot

Shane Douglas

WRESTLECADE – WINSTON-SALEM, NC
NOVEMBER 28, 2015
Jon-Paul Le Blanc - 4 Corners Photography

The Blue Meanie

Animal

Abdullah the Butcher

O.D.B.

Dr. Tom Prichard

Tatanka & the God Father

GULF SOUTH WRESTLING – CHICKASAW, AL
MARCH 23, 2016
Jon-Paul Le Blanc - 4 Corners Photography

Alex Cruz vs. El Fuego

Barry Wolf

Eddie Gilchris & the Minion

Mountain Man vs. K-Quick

The Rainbow Warrior & Lexi

Zane Stevens vs. Airman Banks

CHAMPIONSHIP WRESTLING ASSOCIATION - RIPLEY, MS
MARCH 11, 2016

Jon-Paul Le Blanc - 4 Corners Photography

Johnny Morton vs. Trevor Ballard

Tokyo Monster Kahagas vs. Antonio Garza

Paul Lee & Shane Andrews

Rodney Mack vs. Tracy Smothers

Danny Dollar & Buff Bagwell

Professor P. & Big Ramp

WRESTLECON - DALLAS, TX
APRIL 2, 2016

Jon-Paul Le Blanc - 4 Corners Photography

Adam Asher & Tim Storm

Big Ramp & Su Yung

Tito Santana, Bob Orton Jr., & Sam Roberts

James Beard, Johnny Mantell, & Bruce Tharpe

Vince Russo

Billy Gunn

The Iron Sheik

CENTRAL ALL-STAR – CALLAWAY, FL
JUNE 10, 2016
Jon-Paul Le Blanc - 4 Corners Photography

Matt Gilbert vs. Nathan Beast

John Saxon vs. Drew Game

Jaxson James vs. Beastman

Beastman Wes Fetty & Big Ramp

Fransisco Ciastso & Stormie Lee

Zane Stevens vs. Fransisco Ciatso

HURRICANE PRO – BEAUMONT, TX
JULY 30, 2016
Jon-Paul Le Blanc - 4 Corners Photography

A.J. Rush diving onto Jordan Jenson

Galatica vs. Avarice

Avarice slamming A.J. Rush

Mike Freska stomping Galatica

Rex Andrews drop-kicking Ashton Jacobs

Erik Garza choking Galatica

WRESTLECADE – WINSTON-SALEM, NC
NOVEMBER 26 & 27, 2016
Jon-Paul Le Blanc - 4 Corners Photography

Eric Bicshoff & Sonny Onoo

Randy & Bill Mulkey

Rikishi

Ivan Koloff

Ted DiBiase

Scott Hall

Koko B. Ware

Ricky Steamboat

92

INVASION MUNDIAL LUCHA LIBRE – PELHAM, AL
MARCH 19, 2017
Jon-Paul Le Blanc - 4 Corners Photography

Mike Jackson vs. The Ultimate Dragon

Morgan Fairchild vs. Kiera Hogan

The Ultimate Dragon

Kato Jr. Extreme vs. Oro Jr.

Elimento Independiente

Antonio Garza

Spi Ral

Oro Jr.

VOODOO WRESTLING – BRIDGE CITY, LA
APRIL 15, 2017

Jon-Paul Le Blanc - 4 Corners Photography

Jazz vs. Kendra Hall

El Angel vs. James Comstock

Stan Sweetan vs. Trucker Jones

Minotaur vs. Xtian Blake

Justyn Amazing vs. Trucker Jones

Big Ramp & Mike Chaos

RSWF – MEMPHIS, TN – JUNE 17, 2017
BENEFIT FOR BRICKHOUSE BROWN
Jon-Paul Le Blanc - 4 Corners Photography

Bishop Cage, Nate the Rat Whitlock, Motley Cruz, & Raja

Jimmy Valiant

Vordell Walker vs. John Saxon

Mitch Torreto leg dropping on Gary Valiant

Purple Haze vs. Danny B. Jr.

Reggie B. Phine being choked by Precious

RIVER CITY WRESTLING – SAN ANTONIO, TX
JULY 14, 2017
Wrestleville – Vinny Berry

Katie Forbes vs. Baby D

O.D.B. vs. The Librarian

EC3 vs. The Monster Abyss

La Park vs. Shawn Hernandez

Joey Spector

Michael Faith

POWERSLAM WRESTLING – GULFPORT, MS
DECEMBER 9, 2017
Jon-Paul Le Blanc - 4 Corners Photography

Mustang Mike

Blade Boudreaux vs. Nathan Crown

Joe Kane vs. James Veal

Reggie Matthews vs. Marcus Gibbs

Thunder Blonde vs. Kristen

Thunder Blonde

MAIN EVENT MAINA – NEW ORLEANS, LA
APRIL 7, 2018

Jon-Paul Le Blanc - 4 Corners Photography

Hunter Grey, Titan, & Lance Hoyt

Hunter Grey splashing on Action Jackson

Jaxon Stone vs. Nate Jolly

Cassandra Golden vs. Miranda Alize

Teddy Hart being dropped by Barrett Brown

Estrella Galactica vs. Barrett Brown

CWA WRESTLE RAISE – HOT SPRINGS, AR
MAY 19, 2018
Jon-Paul Le Blanc - 4 Corners Photography

Gary Roosevelt Gram

Brian Christopher & J. Lawler

Mr. Saturday Night

Lex Luger

Brandon White & Bill Dundee

Mike Antohny

Jerry Lawler

Matt Riviera vs. Jerry Lawler

CWA WRESTLE RAISE – HOT SPRINGS, AR
MAY 19, 2018
Jon-Paul Le Blanc - 4 Corners Photography

Greg Anthony vs. Tim Storm

Nate Starr

D' Lo Brown grabbing Barrett Brown

Barrett Brown vs. D' Lo Brown

J.J. Dillon

Action Jackson vs. Dale Wylde

ALL PRO WRESTLING - WHITE CASTLE, LA
JULY 16, 2018
Jon-Paul Le Blanc - 4 Corners Photography

Cody Hawkinz vs. Aski Palomino

Brittany vs. Cassandra Golden

Mustang Mike, Greg Valentine, & Andrew Anderson

Rocket Chris Paul vs. Chris Black

Sean Crow & Eric Garza

Tyson Maddux vs. Robert Godsey

FULL THROTTLE WRESTLING – LAKE CHARLES, LA
SEPTEMBER 22, 2018
Jon-Paul Le Blanc - 4 Corners Photography

Announcer Bryce Boudreaux

Hambone Lee vs. Kore Da' Cajun

Nate Jolly vs. Jared Wayne

Adam Asher vs. T-Ray Watford

Teddy Nail, James Beard,
& Rocket Chris Paul

T.K. Riot vs. Titan

HOODMARK – BRANDON, MS
MAY 5, 2019
Jon-Paul Le Blanc - 4 Corners Photography

Alex Graves vs. Minotaur

Gino Medina vs. El Fuego

Estrella Galactica & Ayden Cristiano

Korey Konstantine vs. Darius Lee

King Garuda

Big Ramp & Matt Cross

REVOLUTION WRESTLING – McALLEN, TX
DECEMBER 28, 2019
Wrestleville – Vinny Berry

Shooter Roberts vs. Vermin

Kon Hawk vs. Jackel

JC Valentine vs. Richard Reason

Criss Austin vs. Matt Riot

Justneph vs. Downtown Felix

Downtown Felix being chopped

PRO WRESTLING 225 - PLAQUEMINE, LA
JANUARY 25, 2020

Jon-Paul Le Blanc - 4 Corners Photography

Announcer Bryce Boudreaux

CJ Cyprian vs. Jordan Jaa

Pillars of Destiny

The Bayou Cartel

Korey Konstantine vs. Rhett Thibodeaux

Marcello Flores is dropkicking Titan

LOKO WRESTLING – HOUSTON, TX
SEPTEMBER 24, 2020
Jon-Paul Le Blanc - 4 Corners Photography

Savage King vs. Diego De la Cruz

Rottweiler Jay Davis vs. Fuego Del Sol

Aaron Zykes dropkicking ASF

Lady Diamond vs. SADIKA

Estrella Galatica & Christi Jaynes

Gino Medina vs. Low Rider

SOUTHERN CHAMPIONSHIP WRESTLING
BAY ST. LOUIS, MS – 11-15-2020
Jon-Paul Le Blanc - 4 Corners Photography

10 bell salute for Hannibal Jaxzin

Sean O'Reilly

Vinny Deniro & Wade HalfBreed Hebert

Vinny Deniro

Thadeus Collins

Seymore Money & Ashton Blake

SOUTHERN CHAMPIONSHIP WRESTLING
KILN, MS – 2-21-2021
Jon-Paul Le Blanc - 4 Corners Photography

High Flying Ace & Wade Half-Breed Hebert

Lord Mitchell Taylor vs. Bobby Joe Bristow

Queen Katelyn kicking Skyler

Steve O'Malley , Vinny
Dinero, & Sean O'Reilly

Mac Daddy Dudds v.s Thaddius Collins

John Taylor

JOHN SAXON

Jon-Paul Le Blanc - 4 Corners Photography

NWA WORLD JR. HEAVYWEIGHT CHAMPION
July 9, 2016 - April 8, 2017

JAMES BEARD – JUNE 19, 2017

Jon-Paul Le Blanc - 4 Corners Photography

James Beard may be one of the more recognized referees in the sport of professional wrestling. He has worked for promotions such as World Class, USWA, Global Wrestling Federation, WWE, and with Super World Sports in Japan for seven years. He is associated with the Cauliflower Alley Club and the Pro Wrestling Hall of Fame, two institutions that are very important to him. James is still known to referee matches almost every weekend.

Though wrestling has been a big part of his life, it was not his first choice for it being his career. In the early 80s, Beard was singing and playing keyboards in a band called Straight Shot. They were being booked by Charlie Pride's production company. Working in nightclubs allowed him to meet an impressive array of people.

"While playing with the band in Dallas and the surrounding areas, I started to get to know some of the wrestlers. They came in and listen to music or I ran into them at different places," James Beard said. "I had gotten to know some of the boys and we started talking about wrestling. They knew I was pretty intelligent about the business and they knew that I wasn't just an average fan."

The wrestlers that he was running into were some of World Class Championship Wrestling's finest superstars. James was rubbing elbows with Kevin and Kerry Von Erich, Bruiser

Brody, and Bill Irwin. Over some time, he became good friends with many of them.

"Brody was one of the guys who was pushing me into it. I got dragged into wrestling," Beard continued. "I wasn't trained, I was talked into it."

James gave into the persuasion of his wrestling friends, and in 1985, he started working part-time as a referee in the sport. At that particular time in his life, he thought he was a little too old to be a wrestler, even though he grew up being athletic. He started by officiating smaller events and some local independent shows around the Dallas and Ft. Worth area. One of his very first matches to officiate was a contest between Bruiser Brody and Abdullah the Butcher. When those two wrestlers stepped into the ring together, they had a reputation for a chaotic wrestling style. Their matches usually ended up outside of the ring for most of the night.

"That was my introduction to the whole thing. Everything was easy after that," Beard laughed. "You didn't have to be too smart to do a match with those two guys. You just had to chase them around and hoped that you didn't get hurt."

From the smaller spot shows that were held at high school gymnasiums, James eventually started working at the bigger venues. Before long is was referring on the World Class events for television. Every Monday, the promotion was in Ft. Worth at the Will Rogers Coliseum, and every Friday night, the matches were held at the Sportatorium in Dallas. The wrestling promotion was a hotbed for talent in the early 1980s. Some will say that December 28th, 1982, was the date that marked a change in the business throughout Texas. On this night, Kerry Von Erich was wrestling Ric Flair for his NWA World Heavyweight Title at Reunion Arena in downtown Dallas. It was a no disqualification match inside a steel cage with specific stipulations. Freebird Michael Hayes was appointed to be a special referee alongside referee David Manning. Freebird Terry Gordy was unofficially assigned by Michael to guard the door of the cage so no one could enter or leave. In the end, Hayes interfered, Flair kept his belt, and Gordy closed the door of the cage on Kerry's head. The war had begun!

"The Freebird and Von Erich feud put World Class Championship Wrestling on the map. It made things beyond exciting there," Beard reminisced. "They hit on the angle with the Freebirds at the right time. It became an incredible experience for the fans."

Not only were the fans engaged in the Freebird – Von Erich feud, but they also watched some epic feuds between Chris Adams and Jimmy Garvin, Iceman King Parsons and Buddy Roberts, Scott Casey and John Tatum, and the Fantastics against the Midnight Express. The territory was on fire and the fans loved it! Attendance at the shows was amazing with almost every event selling out.

"World Class was one of the most unique promotions in the history of the business because of how popular the Von Erich boys were," Beard explained. "So many things were done right and they had so many guys in the right place."

By the time Beard started working for World Class Championship Wrestling in 1985, the promotion started to lose a bit of its luster. This was due to a series of misfortunes that happened during and around that period. One of the first tragedies came when David Von Erich died while on a wrestling tour in Japan on February 10, 1984. David was only 25 years old. Many believed that David had the possibility of one day being the NWA World Heavyweight Champion.

"David was the businessman and he was the guy that could have carried the company forward. He had a good head on his shoulders," Beard stated. "He would have made different business decisions and there is no telling what impact he would have made if he had lived."

The tragedies that followed after David were the deaths of Gino Hernandez, Mike Von Erich, Bruiser Brody, Kerry Von Erich, and Chris Adams. For those who loved the Dallas wrestling scene, it was heartbreaking. A cloud of sadness seemed to cover the state of Texas with each news report.

World Class Championship Wrestling was one of the hottest territories in the 80s. Its peak years were between 1982 and 1985. The National Wrestling Alliance Heavyweight

Champion made frequent visits to wrestle the promotion's top stars. Many of the the popular wrestling magazines covered the Von Erichs and many of their talent regularly.

"I often compare it to Camelot. For that short period, it was the shining star of the wrestling business. It was amazing to be around all of that," Beard sighed. "And because of unfortunate things that happened, it just faded off into obscurity,"

For a time, fans were loyal, and they packed the venues whenever there was a wrestling show. However, as time passed things changed. Month after month, the attendance at the events started to drop, and the mystique that was once so prominent was no longer in existence. No matter how hard the promotion tried to recapture the glory of the past, it did not work. The magic was gone.

By 1990, World Class Championship Wrestling was no longer in business. Matches were still being held at the Sportatorium. Promotions such as USWA, Global Wrestling Federation, NWA, Continental, and New Generation, tried to pick up the pieces when World Class left. The last wrestling television show produced out of the iconic venue was in 1996. That was also the last year that James worked there. The famous building was officially closed in 1998 and demolished in 2003.

"It was pretty sad actually. To this day I think about going to the Sportatorium every Friday night," Beard said. "It's just not an empty lot to me. There's an empty spot in everyone's heart that worked there. It feels like a part of me has been taken away."

Jon-Paul Le Blanc - 4 Corners Photography

James Beard in action - 2018

TRACY SMOTHERS - JUNE 28, 2017

Jon-Paul Le Blanc - 4 Corners Photography

For the past 34 years, Tracy Smothers has been involved in professional wrestling. Now living near Evansville, Indiana, the 54-year-old wrestler still laces up his boots and steps into the ring for a match every chance he gets.

"I don't have to do this. It isn't my job and I am not broke," Tracy Smothers explained. "I pass it on because it was passed on to me. It's our business and it has to be handed down."

When the sport was handed down to Smothers, he was fortunate to have the teachers that he did. When he started his career in 1983, he learned from Stan Lane and Steve Keirn, otherwise known as The Fabulous Ones.

"They were the hottest tag team in the business when I started," Smothers confirmed. "I saw them at the gym and they trained hard. They taught me how to get over with the fans and how to use wrestling psychology."

It was not long after having several training sessions with the Fabulous Ones that Tracy started getting a new set of people to work with. They were his opponents. Smothers found himself in the ring against the likes of Dick Slater, Bob Orton Jr., Dick Murdoch, Bobby Eaton, and Terry Funk.

"How could you not learn from a list of guys like that who had paved the way for so many other wrestlers? They were all phenomenal" Smothers boasted. "They don't make guys like that anymore. I was lucky enough to get into the ring and have a chance to learn from them."

Tracy wrestled in some of the top promotions in the United States. Some of the more recognized companies were Florida Championship Wrestling, Smokey Mountain, WCW, ECW, and the WWF. Smothers has held numerous amount of titles both in single competition and tag team action in almost every place he has wrestled.

Not only has Tracy wrestled throughout the United States, but he has been all over the world too. Smothers has competed in countries such as Germany, England, Wales, Scotland, Ireland, Japan, Malaysia, Australia, and Mexico. All that experience has just added to his wealth of knowledge for "The Wild Eyed Southern Boy.".

"I can't tell you what my favorite promotion was. I liked them all," Smothers responded. "Wrestling gets in your blood. I have gotten to travel to so many different places."

By the time that Smothers had arrived at Extreme Championship Wrestling, he already had been wrestling for nearly 15 years. He wrestled with the faction, The Full Blooded Italians. By his side were Little Guido, Big Sal, and manager, legendary wrestler Tommy Rich. They knew how to work together as a team, take advantage of their opponents, and infuriate the fans.

Smothers and Rich have known each other since 1983. The two men had wrestled with and against each other many times. With Tommy being a veteran of the business, some of his finer points were his psychology for the sport of wrestling. He knew when to do things, how to adlib, and how to sell.

"You need to show the fans your emotions of being mad, glad, happy, or sad. The wrestler needs to show the fan that whatever just happened is affecting them." Smothers affirmed. "Too many of the newer guys today move way too fast."

When Smothers was in his mid 30's and tagging with Guido, he made sure he was doing everything that he could to prepare himself for the intense style of wrestling he was doing. Since he wanted to perform at a high level, Tracy took his training seriously. At that time, there was nothing like ECW. It was a wrestling promotion that changed the business.

"A lot of people think I trained hard because of the hardcore style of wrestling, but it was because of all the talented people that came through there," Smothers responded. "I did weights one day and the other days, I worked out with a boxer, a kickboxer, and a basketball player. I wanted to do what I could to keep up with the younger guys."

Currently, Smothers can be found working on the independent wrestling circuit. He still gets a rush from hearing the cheers and jeers from the crowd. When he is not wrestling, he puts wrestling seminars a few times month for different promotions throughout the country. If a young wrestler is ever in the dressing room with him, there is a good chance that Smothers is willing to teach him.

"I kind of found myself in the role of being somewhat of an agent. I like critiquing the guys on their matches," Smothers added. "For the most part, they are open to my input. I am trying to teach the guys how they can do it better and safer."

TRACY SMOTHERS
September 2, 1962 – October 28, 2020

Jon-Paul Le Blanc - 4 Corners Photography

Jessie Belle & Tracy Smothers in 2016

BILL DUNDEE – AUGUST 15, 2017

Jon-Paul Le Blanc - 4 Corners Photography

Superstar Bill Dundee became a professional wrestler when he was 19 years old. He eventually left his home country of Scotland and wrestled the next 13 years in Australia until meeting fellow wrestler Bobby Shane on a wrestling tour. Shane introduced him to Jerry Jarrett, the booker in the Memphis territory, in 1975. Bill then moved to Tennessee. His epic battles against Jerry Lawler made the Memphis territory one of the hottest in the business. Today at 73, Dundee is still wrestling. His 40 years in the sport as a wrestler and booker have made him one of the more knowledgeable legends in the business. I had a chance to talk to him about the Memphis territory, Jerry Lawler, and the good old days of professional wrestling.

Q: What do you think was so special about the Memphis territory?

A: At the time, Nick Gulas and Roy Welch were the promoters and Jerry Jarrett was the booker. Jerry was so passionate about the wrestling business. He had a knack for looking at a guy and knowing what he could do. He knew who to make a heel and who to make a babyface. A lot of the guys over the years never gave Jerry the accolades that he deserved. When you're a booker, you get a little heat on yourself because a lot of people think that you're not doing the right thing. I thought he was good at it. He was very good to me and also to Jerry Lawler. He booked the two of us in Memphis or wherever else we wrestled, and we made a lot of money and that's what it's all about.

Q: I know that you have done a great deal of booking throughout your career. What do you think someone needs to be successful in that role?

A: You have to believe in what you're doing. I believed that it was real, so I was going to convince the guy in the front row that it was real. We have gotten away from that. I don't know how to put a TV show together just for it to be a silly TV show. I have no idea what to do with a kid flip-flopping all over the place. I would have never done this interview 20 years ago and you wouldn't have been allowed to do it either. But we've exposed the business. Why? I don't know? It's sad what we did to it. You're not talking to a grumpy old man here. I'm 73, but I'm not an old 73. I still work every day and I can still wrestle. I'm not bitter at the wrestling business or at anybody in it. Look at the President of the United States. Donald Trump does wrestling interviews. Politicians didn't act like that, but that's just the world that we live in today. You like Trump or you don't like Trump. You like wrestling or you don't, but we can't tell people that it's real today.

Q: Back in the day, what were some of the things that you guys took into consideration when you were booking matches?

A: In 1976 I went to Jerry Jarrett and I asked him to teach me how to be the booker. It's not as easy as you think it is. Just writing names in a book and putting people in the ring doesn't mean that it's all going to work. Jerry, Eddie Marlin, and I went up and down the roads as we were going to the towns together. We always talked about the business. By doing that, I started to understand how this whole thing worked. It's not a script. I don't know how they do it today, but I know what we did. Nothing was written down except the TV sheet with the times of the matches. We had an hour and a half to do a live show and then we made a 40-minute version of it for cities like Louisville and Evansville. I had to learn it from somebody, and Jerry Jarrett was the one who showed it to me.

Q: Having worked with so many people throughout your career, who do you think that you've learned the most from?

A: Let me put it to you like this. Somebody can teach you the notes and everything when you are singing, but if you don't have the fundamentals of singing you will never be a singer. If you didn't have the fundamentals of wrestling back in the day, you weren't going to be a wrestler. The name of the game is wrestling. It's not stupidity or high flying. It is wrestling and wrestling is done on a mat, but that's not what the kids are doing today. These days, I haven't learned anything from anybody. Hulk Hogan was one of the biggest stars in the wrestling business, but I never learned anything from him. When he was in Memphis, he learned more from me and Jerry Lawler. After that, he went off to be a big star. Good for him. I credit Bobby Shane for taking me under his wing before I came to the United States in 1975. He gave us the fundamentals. I did what he said and here I am 40 years later.

Q: What do you think it was about the chemistry that you had when wrestling against Jerry Lawler?

A: It was the best chemistry in the world. He didn't like me and I didn't like him. It was like we were trying to outshine one another when we went into the ring. We respected each other and we knew what we were doing. Did we break bread every day? No, we didn't. Did we go to the bar at night? No, we didn't. Did we hang around? No, we didn't. We showed up in the town and we wrestled one another and then went our separate ways when it was over. If you have a crown and you're called the King, it means more than someone wearing a jumpsuit and being called a Superstar. That was how we looked at it. I was quite happy being the second fiddle. He was partners with Jerry Jarrett. It's not like you're going to beat the boss. I would have never said things like that 20 years ago and I would have never said that Jerry Lawler owned part of the business.

Q: Was there a particular time that something happened in the business that you thought it wouldn't recover from?

A: Yes, when we lost our television programs. That was what screwed up the territories. Vince hired all the stars from each territory. Hulk Hogan went with them. If you take the star away from the territory, the territory can't survive and that's what happened. Lawler and I both stayed in Memphis and that territory stayed around the longest time. Eventually, Lawler went to work for Vince and how can you blame him? He was getting a big paycheck every week. It was just business. The territories eventually died. That's what happened.

Q: Now that all the independent promotions are coming up in the United States, do you think that the territory system might be coming back?

A: No, it is not coming back. For one thing, you need a TV show. Nobody's got one except Vince. We just can't blame Vince for the state that wrestling is in today. It just wasn't him. There are more millionaire wrestlers today and more billionaire promoters than there were back in the day. We all made a good living, but not what it's like today. Every time a John Wayne movie comes on TV, I sit down and watch it, but I've already seen it a hundred times. It's John Wayne though, and I like what he did. Without TV you can't do anything, especially on the local level. Memphis was the most-watched TV show ever on Saturday morning. There was nobody else in the United States that had an hour and a half of live wrestling at that time.

Q: Did you ever think that you would still be wrestling today?

A: I never made it hard on my body. I started in Judo and the very first thing they teach you in Judo is to break your fall. You learn how to take the bump. I was taught to take the bumps on my feet. My feet were like the shock absorbers for a car. We were taught to get our legs down first. I have never had any back problems. I trained to have a long career. I am 73, and I am the toughest 73-year old that you will ever meet. David believed he could whoop Goliath before he went out and whooped him.

Q: Do you think the wrestlers of today are taking more risks than they have to, and as a result, they are suffering more injuries?

A: Yes, because mainly they can't wrestle. The name of the game is wrestling. It hasn't changed in the last 100 years. It says wrestling on the marquee. It isn't called bumps and acrobatics. Wrestling today is a circus act. They all think it's great, but if you can't fight, what's it going to do for you. I'm not saying the kids today aren't athletic, they are, but they aren't wrestling.

Q: Today I know WWE has writers. What are they writing? Are they writing the story lines or are they writing what the wrestlers have to say?

A: I don't know. If they are writing what the wrestlers are saying, that's probably why they can't talk. When I did an interview, I hit the points that I wanted to say. If I was wrestling the big fat guy, that was part of my interview. "How is that guy going to beat me, he can hardly walk because he weighs 300 pounds." "He's so fat he won't be able to catch me." "I would run around him so fast that he'll think he's surrounded." It was just stuff that I was coming up with at the moment and it was coming from my heart. I don't know how they do it today. I have never been to one of Vince's shows to see them put it together. The closest I ever got, was the time I went up to Vince's house about 20 years ago. We talked, but I guess I didn't talk right to him because now I'm talking to you from Memphis, Tennessee. My job with Vince never materialized. That's another story. Randy Savage and I never really saw eye to eye back then. The Undertaker and I never really saw eye to eye back then either. They were his top stars, so he wasn't going to put some little five-foot-seven guy in there to stir up some trouble with them. Do you know what I mean? If they didn't want you there, you weren't going to be there.

Q: What do you think it's going to take to get wrestling back to the way that it was?

A: It's done. It's over. John Wayne isn't coming back. When I was a kid, John Wayne was the man, and then Clint Eastwood came up and started making western movies. After that, the days of the West were over. Wrestling has gone the same way I'm afraid. Promoters like Eddie Graham, Jerry Jarrett, Verne Gagne, and all the people that promoted and loved wrestling are all gone. So, the kids today that are becoming promoters don't have a clue, and they'll book anybody to wrestle for ten dollars.

FUN FACTS
Favorite opponent: Jerry Lawler
Career highlight: The 30-foot scaffold match with Koko B. Ware.
Favorite sports team: Dallas Cowboys
Hobbies: Riding motorcycles
Dog person or cat person: Dog person
Favorite Food: Steak and eggs
A movie you have seen multiple times: Pick any John Wayne movie.
Favorite actor: John Wayne
Favorite color: Pink and black.

Jon-Paul Le Blanc - 4 Corners Photography
Bill Dundee with Jimmy Valiant in 2015

BROWN FULLFILLS DREAM – AUGUST 29, 2017

Photo Courtesy of Barrett Brown

Barrett Brown accomplished his lifelong wrestling dream by winning the NWA Junior Heavyweight Title on August 12, 2017, from Mr. USA in Dyersburg, Tennessee. The 23-year-old from Seven Points, Texas had wrestled for the prestigious belt back in 2012, but Brown came up short. Five years later, with the belt in his possession, he is ready to take on the world! Wrestleville had a chance to talk to him about his match, his win, and his future plans.

Q: What does it mean for you to have won the NWA Junior Heavyweight World Title?

A: It's a dream come true. It is something I have worked my entire adult life for. It is something that goes back to my original trainer (Cody Cunningham), and it was something that we had always talked about. We said if I was ever to win this championship that my career would have come full circle and all our work would have paid off. It's a huge responsibility that comes along with holding this championship, and it's one that I am willing to take on. Everything just came full circle for me.

Q: When you look at the list of names that have held that title before you, what goes through your mind?

A: It is humbling. When I see names like Danny Hodge, Verne Gagne, and Chavo Guerrero Sr., it blows my mind. I was looking at the Wikipedia page after the match and it was already updated that night. To see my name on that list with those guys is very humbling.

Q: Was this the first time that you wrestled Mr. USA? What kind of opponent was he?

A: It was the first time that we had ever met. I think the match went about 12 or 15 minutes. We were the main event at NWA Mid-South in Dyersburg, Tennessee. The match was competitive and it went back and forth. He's is a very good opponent and was a deserving champion.

Q: Is there talk about defending the title in a rematch against him any time soon?

A: Not currently. Mr. USA and I had talked about it after our match, but there is nothing set at this time.

Q: It has been five years since you had the opportunity to wrestle for the NWA Junior title. What did it feel like waiting for such a long time to get another shot at that belt?

A: It felt like an eternity. I had my first shot when I was only 18 years old. It was humbling just to be able to say that I was able to wrestle for that belt. It feels like everything has finally paid off.

Q: Now that you are Champion, do you think that you're going to be fighting tougher competition?

A: Absolutely. I know for sure that my very first championship defense is going to be on September 16th in Arkansas against Chavo Guerrero Jr. He is going to be a worthy opponent for that championship. It's historic because I know that his father also held the same championship. It's going to be very cool to defend the belt to a former Champion's son.

Q: Now that you are a champion what can we expect from you?

A: I don't want to be one of those wrestlers that disrespect the championship. Being a champion comes along with the responsibility to raise the prestige of this championship as much as possible. Anytime that the NWA can find an opponent for me, I will defend it as much as possible, and I will travel as far as I have to. I will wrestle against the best in the world just to prove that I am a worthy champion. I want to make this championship a household name.

Q: When you look at the current NWA title holders, what does it mean for you to know that you are associated with that same class of Champions?

A: Tim Storm is someone who I consider to be my wrestling Godfather. He has taught me so much and has given me so much advice over the last five years. All the advice that he has given me has helped me grow so much. The fact that he and I are both the World Heavyweight Champion and the World Junior Heavyweight Champion at the same time, is very special to me.

Q: When we talked the first time, you said that if you ever were to win the NWA Junior Heavyweight Title, you would take it to show your original trainer Cody Cunningham. Have you had a chance to do that yet?

A: Yes I did. I won the championship on Saturday and Sunday I traveled back home. That night, I got in touch with him, and I met him at his house so he could see it. It was such a good moment and he was close to tears because I had won it. Everything that we had ever talked about had finally come true. It was a really good moment.

FUN FACTS
Favorite wrestler: Shawn Michaels
Career highlight: Winning the NWA Junior Title
Favorite band: Aerosmith
Favorite sports team: Dallas Cowboys
Hobbies: Traveling, working out, and playing video games.
Dog person or cat person: Dog person
A state you have never been to: Wyoming and Rhode Island.
Favorite food: Pizza
Favorite actor: Tom Hardy
Favorite color: Blue

RICKY MORTON – SEPTEMBER 10, 2017

Jon-Paul Le Blanc - 4 Corners Photography

Robert Gibson & Ricky Morton

When it comes to wrestling tag teams, no two men have left an impression on the sport quite like the Rock 'n' Roll Express have. In their multi-decade careers, along with holding the NWA World Tag Team Championship belts, Ricky Morton and Robert Gibson have held more championships together than one person could ever imagine. Their accomplishments, charisma, and in-ring ability, have secured their place in the history books. They are one of the best teams to ever have stepped in the ring. Their epic feud with the Midnight Express, and their historic scaffold matches against them, are some of the high points that the Rock n' Roll Express has experienced. No highlight in their long career, however, compares to what happened on March 31st, 2017.

"When Robert and I were inducted into the WWE Hall of Fame, it was one of the greatest things that ever happened to us in our business. A lot of people said that it couldn't be a real hall of fame without the Rock 'n' Roll Express in it," Ricky Morton said. "That was everything that Robert and I had worked for, and we were never treated any better in our lives."

Today, the 61-year-old wrestler still sees action inside the ring. Ricky's passion for the business has helped him steer his priorities into another direction, teaching the younger generation the sport of wrestling. These days, coaching gives him a great deal of satisfaction. After spending 44 years in the wrestling business, he has a wealth of knowledge that benefits any willing wrestling student.

"It's just something that you do when you know the business as I do. You pass it on," Morton continued. "I think the art of wrestling has been lost, and that's why I opened the School of Morton. It helps with the bills, however, everything we make goes back into the school."

The School of Morton is located in Chucky, Tennessee, which is 80 miles east of Knoxville. The facility has been opened since January of 2014, and currently, has between 40 to 50 students enrolled. Along with Ricky, the school is run by his partner James Strange and Strange's wife Lisa.

"They have come up with a lot of good ideas for the school and hopefully, it will all pay off for us," Morton replied. "It's hard to get a business going and to keep it going. The school is more than just about wrestling for me, I teach a lot of kids there too."

Even though he gets some criticism for having a young clientele, that aspect is one of the main things that help the School of Morton stand out. Ricky does not just teach your average young adult who is in their late teens or early 20's. He also teaches children and whoever else wants to learn how to wrestle safely and in a professional manner. He has even taught children with disabilities.

"I love teaching them about our wrestling business, but I'm also able to teach them about the mistakes that I made in my life," Morton explains. "I'm not a doctor, I'm not a genius, I'm not a philosopher or a teacher, but I do want to teach them how important their education is. I have young kids and I get a lot of flak for it, but you have to understand we're in the entertainment business."

Over the past couple of decades, independent wrestling promotions have been popping up all over the country. Most promoters today are trying to do business the right way, but Ricky has heard stories of promoters lying to sponsors and lying to the fans. He has even seen himself advertised on posters for shows that he was not hired to wrestle on. Most of the shows that he sees today, in his opinion, are not worth going to due to the lack of knowledge and professionalism that is being practiced.

"When fans go and watch these shows that are so horrible, they think that the entire business is like that. It's hard to overcome things like this especially when you're on the independent circuit," Morton expressed. "This is not a joke to me, but you got a lot of guys that have about as much business in the ring as I do flying the space shuttle."

The main reason why Ricky wanted to open up the School of Morton was that he loves wrestling, and he got tired of watching people disrespect the business. Wrestling is all that he has ever done, and he has been committed to it for the last 44 years of his life. If there is anything that needs to be said about Ricky Morton and his ability in training successful wrestlers, being one half of the Rock 'n' Roll Express should be able to speak for itself.

"To be a good wrestler you have to put a hundred percent of your life into it," Morton says. "There is no second place. Second place means you're a loser, and if you put everything you got into this business, it will pay off in the long run."

Jon-Paul LeBlanc - 4 Corners Photography

The Rock N' Roll Express

SHAWN HERNANDEZ - SEPTEMBER 25,2017

Wrestleville – Vinny Berry

Super Mex Shawn Hernandez may have never had a permanent role in WWE, but the man from Houston, Texas is a global superstar. The passion and dedication that he has had for wrestling over the last 20 years have allowed him to secure a place in the sport. In that time, he maintained professional and personal success. Not every independent wrestler can do that. Most wrestlers struggle on the independent circuit until they get their big break, and are offered the dream spot with the WWE. Hernandez however, is not like most wrestlers. Aside from having a few dark matches with the largest wrestling promotion in the world, Super Mex never wanted to be a full-time wrestler on the WWE roster.

"I was more captivated by the Lucha wrestling and the Japanese style. I found it more appealing to be able to say that I'm going to Australia for three months, or I'm going to Germany for two months," Shawn Hernandez commented. "I wanted to do my job and then go home. It was never my dream to be on RAW or Smackdown every week."

Professional wrestling is physically and mentally demanding. To be successful in the long run, one needs to possess certain character attributes. If you are missing athleticism or discipline, you are in the wrong business. Growing up, Hernandez was fortunate to have both. Shawn's father was a Green Beret who served in the Viet Nam War. His 30-year military experience had a huge influence on Shawn and though his father was very loving, he was also very strict. Shawn was expected to achieve passing grades. He was not allowed to play football until the 11th grade and his first date was at his senior prom.

High school football prepared him for a defensive spot on two different college teams. However, when it came to the NFL, no team was looking for a 260-pound defensive lineman. When college ended, he passed on the Canadian Football League after having a tryout. Hernandez came back to Houston and played two years with the Arena Football League. But at the age of 25, with the responsibility of supporting a child, Hernandez knew that Arena Football was not going to be his golden ticket. At a crossroads in his life and not knowing what he was going to do, he decided to pursue his childhood dream. He wanted to become a professional wrestler.

"It was a little awkward because I was 25 and I was asking my father for permission," Hernandez explained. "Football didn't pay the bills and it was important for my father to raise me as a productive member of society."

Hernandez did not have to go far to get professional training. He trained with Tugboat and Chaz Taylor in his hometown of Houston. When the time was right, he hit the independent scene hard. By 1999, he was working regularly with Texas All-Star Wrestling. After holding the mid-card spot for three months, he moved up to having main event matches. It was also around the time when Shawn had some dark matches with the WWE and had a couple of tours to Japan.

"Wrestling regularly and making decent money is two different things," Hernandez replied. "It was about this time that I thought that I could break out and make some money at this."

Wrestling outside the United States and establishing himself as an international wrestler in countries such as Germany, Australia, Japan, and Mexico, enabled him to be a full-time wrestler. When Shawn came back to the States, he struggled to make substantial money wrestling on the weekends on the independent circuit.

"Nobody was teaching me how to make money regularly. They were happy to see me fly off the top rope, but I couldn't make money wrestling on those small shows," Hernandez said. "I was told that I needed to do transitional wrestling, mat wrestling, and I needed to have excellent conditioning."

Shawn became willing to humble himself. For an entire year, Hernandez made the round trip drive from Houston to Atlanta to work with NWA Wildside. It was there he learned how to polish his craft. The promotion had a proven track record. Wrestlers such as New Jack, Ron Killings, C.W. Anderson, and A.J. Styles, came through there on occasion. At the time, Bill Behrens was in charge, under his guidance and the help of the wrestlers on his roster, Shawn was determined to grow as a technician in the sport of wrestling.

"The biggest paycheck that I received while I wrestled at NWA Wildside was $30.00. But if I hadn't done that, I still wouldn't be making any money on the weekends," Hernandez affirmed. "After that, I got my first opportunity to wrestle in Puerto Rico and by 2003; I had my first run in TNA."

The TNA stint in 2003 did not last long, but in 2006, Shawn was with the company once more. His run the second time lasted off and on up until 2014. Hernandez enjoyed his time with TNA because the wrestling promotion filmed four episodes in a six to 10 day period. That schedule allowed him to keep his international wrestling dates. Most importantly, however, TNA was Shawn's first significant exposure to a mass audience.

"Being a national TV star is what every wrestler dreams of," Hernandez answered. "TNA didn't have a developmental system, so I needed to be ready before I got on TV."

Even though Hernandez lacked the knowledge of how to wrestle for the television cameras, he was in luck. His friend and LAX tag team partner Homicide, not only shared ownership of the NWA and TNA tag belts, but he also became Shawn's teacher.

"He told me to listen to him so I could get through the match. Later, he explained to me how and why we did things a certain way," Hernandez recalls. "He became my mentor, brother, and friend. I spent more time with him on the road than I did with my own family sometimes."

Today at the age of 44, Super Mex is still experiencing his share of in-ring action. Along with his regularly scheduled trips to Japan and Europe, Shawn has hooked up with Lucha Libre AAA Worldwide, based out of Mexico City, Mexico. His affiliation with the promotion offers him television exposure, the opportunity to work with top talent, and the chance for him to continue doing what he loves to do. Wrestling is a time-limited sport and Shawn is well aware of that. He feels if he cannot consistently perform at a high level and he becomes more of a liability, it will be time to hang up his gear.

"I told myself long ago when I can't do the Superman dive off the top rope anymore, that I will call it quits," Hernandez said. "Most of the fans are young, and nobody wants to see their heroes get old."

FUN FACTS
Favorite wrestler: La Park and Ric Flair.
Career highlight: Winning the TNA tag belts the first time
Favorite sports team: UNC Tar Heels
Hobbies: Working out
Dog person or cat person: Dog person
Favorite food: Sushi
A movie that you've seen multiple times: V for Vendetta

Photo by Wrestleville
Shawn Hernandez - McAllen, Texas in 2017

MIKE RAPADA – OCTOBER 2, 2017

Photo Courtesy of Mike Rapada

Mike Rapada was 27 years old when he broke into the wrestling business, but after he got there, he stayed. You can still find him inside of the ring. The 53-year-old wrestler who bears the nickname The Colorado Kid can still be found on the independent scene. He has spent the past eight years wresting in the southern and central areas of the United States.

"Today, wrestling is about me entertaining myself. It's not like I'm trying to get anywhere because I've already done all that," Mike Rapada explained. "I'm trying to help out the younger kids and get them where they want to go."

If wrestlers are willing to listen to the Colorado Kid, they just might have a chance to go somewhere in wrestling. When Rapada came up the ranks, he was determined to be a successful wrestler. His accomplishments credited to his name have proven he has done just that. He has wrestled with the WWE, WCW, the NWA, and all over of the world.

"Back in the day, I didn't feel comfortable having drinks and stuff like that. Everybody thought I was stuck up," Rapada replied. "I just wanted to protect what I had worked so hard for. Now, I will have some drinks with the boys and they think I'm pretty cool, but I was cool back then too."

Many wrestlers dream of winning the NWA World Heavyweight Title, but few ever get the chance to wear the precious 10 pounds of gold around their waist. Rapada has held that championship on two different occasions. His first title reign started on September 19, 2000, when he defeated Jerry Flynn in a tournament. That tenure lasted only 56 days after Rapada was defeated by Sabu in Tampa, Florida. On December 22nd of that same year, Rapada faced Sabu once more, and the two battled themselves into a bloody mess in Nashville, Tennessee. To say this match was a classic example of technical wrestling was the furthest thing from the truth. It was an all-out war! In the end, the Colorado Kid persevered and won the title back.

"Sabu is a crazy wrestler and he's just coming at you. You have to just grit your teeth and hope he hurts himself more than he hurts you," Rapada said. "He put duct tape on his arm after severely cutting it on a table to prevent the loss of blood just so he could finish the match."

On that title reign, Mike held the championship for four months before losing it to Steve Corino on April 21, 2001. Sharing space on the same historic list with such notable wrestlers like Lou Thesz, Ric Flair, Dusty Rhodes, Dan Severn, and Kerry Von Erich, is special for Rapada. Besides all that, something else means more to him than being recognized as the National Wrestling Alliance's top man. He has also held the NWA North American Heavyweight Championship. Rapada has held that belt on five different occasions, between 1998 and 2000. On his last reign as the North American Champ, he did not lose the belt, it was vacated due to him winning the NWA's elite prize.

"Being the North American Heavyweight Champion showed me more good times. There were more good memories attached to that than the World belt had," Rapada mentioned. "When I got the world belt, it was almost like the beginning of the end. I found out that there's more to wrestling than just making it to the top."

Another very special moment in Mike's career came in 2003. The NWA invited him to be a part of a wrestling event in China. Rapada was one of the first Americans to ever wrestle in that country. It was a thrill for him to wake up the next morning and see himself on the front of the sports page drop kicking his opponent.

"I was speaking with a diplomat from the Chinese government and he had an interpreter," Rapada commented. "I'm from a little bitty small town and someone paid money to listen to what I had to say. I've been able to experience a lot of things people don't get to."

In the beginning, Mike was extremely fortunate to have good trainers that saw potential in him. They all thought he could make a career out of it. Guys like Eddie Marlin and Jerry and Jeff Jarrett taught him the fundamentals that ultimately honed his skills. It was Kenny Wayne however, who helped Rapada shape his character.

"He told me how to carry myself and how I needed to act. He also told me to keep my nose clean, and not let the other guys block my path. He told me not to be stupid," Rapada articulated. "I didn't expect all of the things that happened to me regarding my career, but when they did, I remembered Kenny. I knew how to wrestle, but Kenny taught me how to be a wrestler."

Wrestling is not just something that Mike Rapada does, it is something that he is a part of, and it is a part of him. He believes that when wrestling is performed correctly, it can be a masterpiece. Mike is the artist painting a picture and telling his story. Throughout his career, he has seen his share of good days and bad.

In his 26 years as a professional wrestler, he has found out that not everyone gets into wrestling for the same reasons or for the right reasons. Some people just want to fight, some want to win, and others want to kiss the girls and hug the babies. Rapada has come across many people in the sport who are apathetic to what happens on the mat. Mike has a strong belief when it comes to wrestling.

"I hope that the fans feel like I did things the right way, and I hope they didn't feel like they were left out," Rapada said. "I realize that I couldn't have done it without my fans, my friends, my family, and the people that supported me."

FUN FACTS
Favorite wrestler: Randy Savage
Career highlight: Wrestling in China in 2003.
Favorite band: Bon Jovi
Favorite sports team: L.A. Chargers
Hobbies: Bike riding and playing golf.
Dog person or cat person: Dog person, cat person, and a bird person.
A state that you've never been to: Alaska and Hawaii
Favorite food: Authentic Mexican food
Movie I've seen multiple times: Jaws
Favorite actor: Arnold Schwarzenegger
Favorite color: Orange

Photo Courtesy of Mike Rapada

NWA WORLD HEAVYWEIGHT CHAMPION
1ST: September 19, 2000- November 14, 2000
2ND: December 22, 2000 - April 24, 2001

ANTHONY RETURNS – OCTOBER 9, 2017

Jon-Paul Le Blanc - 4 Corners Photography

Golden Boy Greg Anthony has stepped in the ring with some very tough opponents over the years. A few of his biggest battles were against guys like Billy Gunn, Zach Gowen, and Jerry Lawler, but nothing prepared Anthony for the battle he had gone through this past June. The 36-year-old from Dyersburg, Tennessee found out that he had been wrestling with a severe heart problem for about a year. While in the ring with his opponents, Greg started to experience pains in his chest and he became concerned that it could be something serious. After he was urged by his friend Matt Riviera to go see a doctor, Greg took his advice and went.

"I thought the pains that I was having in my chest were because of my weight or maybe it was being caused by having high blood pressure," Greg Anthony said. "What I found out was that I had a 90% blockage in one artery, and 70% blockage in two others."

Greg received the news about his heart condition on Friday, June 16th, just one day before being scheduled to wrestle Tim Storm for the NWA World Heavyweight Championship. The Golden Boy was advised not to go forward with the bout and the doctors scheduled him to have surgery on the following Tuesday. Due to where the blockages were located in Greg's heart, the medical team was not sure if they needed to do a quadruple by-pass, or if they could use stents to fix the clogged arteries. The decision was determined in the operating room, and fortunately, stents took care of his problem.

"I could feel immediate relief when I got out of surgery," Anthony stated." I could breathe and it felt like I had more oxygen."

There is no doubt that Greg made the right decision, although the timing of things could have been better. He ultimately had to step down from one of the most important matches of his career. Greg believes that if he did not have the surgery that he would have died.

"I was wrestling 30-minute matches twice a week with a 90% blockage for almost a year," Anthony replied. "The doctors couldn't believe I was able to do what I did in the condition I was in."

Most importantly, Greg did not suffer any other damage to his heart. Now that the surgery is behind him and the blockages have been taken care of, he is focusing on his recovery and getting back into the ring. Greg was in cardiac rehab for six weeks and eventually started working out in the gym on his own. All that time, he thought about one thing, and that is being able to wrestle Simon Reed for the Unified Heavyweight Title. The match is scheduled for this Saturday at "Glory Lasts Forever III," in Dyersburg, Tennessee.

"I consider myself pound for pound and inch per inch, the best in professional wrestling. I was wrestling a breath away from a heart attack," Anthony mentioned. "Now, I am going to be better. I'm going to be a better performer, a better man, and a better everything."

As for Simon Reed, he and Greg are no strangers to each other. Reed is a member of the Office, which is led by Christopher White. Their faction has vowed to put Greg out of professional wrestling for good. Greg has plans for Reed when they step into the ring in a couple of days.

"He will get to see four months of frustration. I have wrestled all of my adult life and there has never been a time I haven't been wrestling," Anthony explained. "These past four months have been the toughest time of my life because I have had to sit back and do nothing."

When Greg Anthony returns to the ring this Saturday night, he will not have to sit back any longer. Returning to the ring is the only thing on his mind and Reed had better watch out. The fans will be reminded once again what they have known all of these years, that Greg Anthony is a force to be reckoned with and he has a heart of gold!

Jon-Paul Le Blanc - 4 Corners Photography

Greg Anthony vs. Matt Boyce in 2018

CHRIS MICHAELS - OCTOBER 29, 2017

Photo Courtesy of Chris Michaels

Professional wrestling has carved out a spot for Chris Michaels. Sure, he has put in a lot of hard work, but he believes that wrestling is his destiny. The 44-year-old wrestler from Franklin, Kentucky, has been in and around the sport almost his entire life. The path that he is traveling on today was laid out for him a long time ago when he was just a young boy.

"When I was growing up, wrestling was a pastime for me and my mother. We used to watch the old Memphis wrestling with Jerry Lawler and Bill Dundee from the Jarrett promotions every Saturday morning," Chris Michaels explained. "My mother took me to the matches if they came close to where we lived. That's how I got hooked on it."

Chris was a typical kid while growing up. He was athletic and he liked to play baseball. When he was a teenager, he taught himself how to play the drums, and then he had aspirations of wanting to be a rock star. When he was 16, Chris met a new girl at school and that changed everything for Chris.

"She told me that her father was a former wrestler who had plans to open up a school," Michaels said. "I told her that I wanted to talk to her dad."

Chris quickly met his new friend's father, who eventually became his trainer. His name was Bill Crockett, who wrestled professionally in the '60s and '70s. Chris talked to his mother and she was behind her son all the way. She helped Chris come up with the $1,000.00 down payment so he could start training.

The rest of the money could be made in payments. His mother had to sign a waiver for him just in case he got hurt since he was still a minor.

"We trained on Wednesdays and Sundays and Bill ended up giving me a key. I could go up there and fiddle around anytime I wanted to," Michaels mentioned. "Some of the other trainees came in and I got in there and worked out with them. Sometimes, some veteran wrestlers showed up so they could knock off some ring rust."

One of the guys who came by to use the facility was Tracy Smothers. By that time, it was around 1990. Tracy had already been wrestling professionally for about seven years and Chris was just starting out. The two men struck up a friendship.

"He thought that I was a talented kid and that I might go somewhere in this business. We swapped numbers and he told me to call him anytime," Michaels replied. "If it wasn't for Tracy taking me under his wing, I wouldn't have gotten to do some of the things I have done. He gave me the knowledge I needed for the wrestling business."

Chris was eager to make a name in the sport and that was what he set out to do. The young man from Kentucky wrestled throughout the south and got connected with wrestling promotions such as USWA, Smokey Mountain Wrestling, WCW, and Music City Wrestling. In those promotions, he learned everything he could. In 1999, almost 10 years after meeting Tracy Smothers, the two wrestlers had the opportunity to work alongside each other for the next four years. It was during that time they spent time working at OVW and the WWE.

"I don't think I could have picked up everything I needed to know about the business without Tracy helping me," Michaels said. "During 1999 and 2002, we made a ton of money because we stayed so busy and he made sure that I was taken care of."

In a business where individuals seem to be fighting for the top spot in the main event, Tracy taught Chris the importance of helping others. He did not do it just by telling him, he did it by showing him. Chris could have figured things out on his own, but with Tracy's help, it happened that much faster.

"I have patterned my career after his in the way that he has always been willing to help others," Michaels replied. "I respect everything about Tracy. He has always been willing to help guys get better and help guys get bookings."

After 25 years Chris and Tracy are still friends. The two wrestlers still occasionally work together. You can find Chris almost every Friday night at the New South Arena in Franklin, Kentucky.

"It's great because it's within walking distance from where I live," Michaels commented. "If there is ever a time I can't find a babysitter, I just take the kids to the matches."

Through the years, Chris has learned how to live and survive working in a business that not everyone can adapt to. There have been ups and downs throughout his career, but wrestling has been a consistent component of his life.

"I have gotten to do a lot of things in the wrestling business that I am very proud of," Michaels explained. "I owe just about all of my success in wrestling to Tracy."

Photo Courtesy of Chris Michaels

Chris Michaels & Tracy Smothers in 2017

FUN FACTS
Favorite wrestler: Ric Flair
Career highlight: It's hard to pick just one.
Favorite band: Kiss
Favorite sports team: Dallas Cowboys
Hobbies: Spending time with the family.
Dog person or cat person: Dog person.
A state that you've never been to: Connecticut
Favorite food: Grilled chicken
The movie I've seen multiple times: The Rocky movies.
Favorite actor: Sylvester Stallone
Favorite color: Red
My dream match: Kurt Angle
A book I've read: The Gene Simons
autobiography, "Kiss & Makeup"
Favorite Dessert: Strawberry cheesecake ice cream.

Photo Courtesy of James Carver

Mr. USA & Chris Michaels - May 19, 2017

CHASE OWENS – NOVEMBER 6, 2017

Photo Courtesy of Chase Owens

Professional wrestler Chase Owens has worked for New Japan Pro Wrestling for the past three years. Since 2015, he's been associated with the Bullet Club. In wrestling, the Bullet Club name is held in high regard. Several of the top name athletes in the sport have wrestled in that faction. The Bullet Club is a group of foreign wrestlers that work in Japan and are determined to dominate the scene there. Men like Kenny Omega, Prince Devitt (Finn Balor), A.J. Styles, Luke Gallows, Adam Cole, and Tanga Loa are some of the wrestlers that have helped secure this elite club's name in the wrestling history books.

"To me, those are some of the most talented guys that I've ever been around," Chase Owens explained. "Being a part of it has helped my career and I'm very grateful for that."

The Bullet Club has been compared to the legendary NWO from the WCW days. The members of the exclusive group tend to wrestle with a chip on their shoulders. They make their presence known every time they step inside the ring. The popularity that is associated with the Bullet Club has far exceeded Japan. It has spread worldwide.

"I think the Bullet Club is one of the hottest things going in professional wrestling today, and it seems like everybody's talking about it," Owens mentioned. "I can hardly go out of the house without seeing a Kenny Omega or a Bullet Club shirt."

The 27-year-old grappler from Bristol, Virginia, has been wrestling since he was 16. After being in the business for only nine months, Chase had the good fortune of meeting Ricky Morton, one half of the Rock N' Roll Express. Morton was impressed with the teenager's in-ring performance and asked Chase if he wanted to start traveling with him.

"He was getting me booked on all these shows with him every night," Owens continued "After the shows, he told me what needed to work on and what I could to do better."

Getting advice from Ricky Morton is something special, but that was not the only veteran wrestler that played a role in Chase's career. While he and Ricky traveled from show to show, one of the guys who rode with them was a former member of the Midnight Express, Bobby Eaton. Morton and Eaton are true legends of the sport and the two of them share the wealth of knowledge for anyone wanting to succeed in the profession.

"I was able to learn from two of the best in this business. Ricky and Bobby helped me with the details of wrestling and what make the matches great," Owens replied. "They taught me about storytelling in the ring."

After wrestling for more than a decade, Owens has had many memorable moments throughout his career. On October 12th, 2012, Owens won the NWA Jr. Heavyweight Title, which was the first of three title reigns he ultimately achieved. That first win will stay with Owens for the rest of his life.

"It was a special accomplishment for me, even though the NWA isn't what it was back in the day," Owens said. "It's an incredible feeling to be on that list with some of the greatest wrestlers of all times."

While Owens was champion, the NWA had a working relationship with Japan, and that was one of the first steps that eventually led to him working in that country. Wrestling in Japan for Owens was always his goal; however on January 4th, 2014 in Kingsport, Tennessee he had one of his all-time dream matches. What made that night so special is that Owens was in the ring defending the NWA Jr. Heavyweight Title to his mentor. For most of Ricky's career, he shared in tag team action with his partner Robert Gibson. On this night, however, he was going for the gold all by himself. In the end, Ricky defeated Chase, becoming the holder of the prestigious belt.

"Being a part of Ricky's win in his first singles world title was not only a great moment for him, but it was a great moment for me as well," Owens stated. "Holding a major singles title was something he has never done before. I was glad to share that moment with him."

When Chase is not in Japan, he is wrestling on the weekends in the United States. Wrestling is something he loves, and something that Chase takes very serious. When he is not wrestling, you can find him with new wrestlers, doing for them what Ricky has done for him.

"I feel like it's my job to continue passing along the knowledge that was passed on to me," Owens said. "I want to carry forward the vision Ricky has for professional wrestling by teaching new students."

T & T Wrestling Photos

Chase Owens vs. Hooks - Addyston, Ohio in 2018

TIM STORM - NOVEMBER 16, 2017

Jon-Paul Le Blanc - 4 Corners Photography

On Sunday, November 12th, NWA World Heavyweight Champion Tim Storm successfully defended his belt against Nick Aldis a 14 year veteran of the business. The match took place near Los Angeles, California, hosted by Championship Wrestling from Hollywood. The match garnered significant media hype and was probably just what new owner Billy Corgan was hoping for after he officially took over the historic wrestling promotion back in October. Wrestleville talked to Tim about the match and his thoughts about his future with the NWA moving ahead.

Q: How does it feel to be the current NWA World Champion considering all the changes that have taken place since the new ownership?

A: Every day is Christmas for me. Every day that I wake up and know that I am the NWA's World Champion, is another great day for me. This is more than what I have ever expected and more than what a lot of people expected. There are a lot of people that say I deserve it, and there are a lot of people that say I don't. That's not for me to determine. All I can do is my best in the situations that I'm put in. I'm very blessed and thankful that I am getting this opportunity and that's how I'm going to approach everything. I get up every day, eat right, go to the gym, and prepare for my next title defense.

Q: What did it mean for you to successfully defend your title against Nick Aldis with the match being broad-casted live on Facebook?

A: I didn't know it was going to be broad-casted live on Facebook. It would have been the same match either way. Nick Aldis is phenomenal. He is one of the best I've ever been in the ring with. I see a skill level that I haven't seen in a long time and Nick was a serious challenge. Nick has to be one of the top unsigned independent free agents out there right now.

Q: Why do you think Nick is so good?

A: In his own words, he was thrown into the spotlight at a very young age with some of the top names in the business. He benefited from that and took full advantage of it. His knowledge and his skill level are what strike me. I don't know why he isn't under contract in New York or somewhere else. He is very impressive. I experienced some things in the ring with him that I haven't experienced in my 20 years of wrestling. It was a learning experience for me, and I'm going to be better because of it.

Q: What kind of response have you gotten in regards to the match from the fans and your peers?

A: It was an old-school NWA match and we told a good story. The match took place in a small ring with two big guys. We both got tangled up in the ropes a little bit. I think Nick said that I got an advantage from the ropes and he is questioning the finish. My response to that is yes, the ropes were something we ran into, and if anything, it was a disadvantage. I got tangled up in them too. I'm proud of the match. That was 3 days ago, and I still feel like I was hit by a semi-truck. Some people were critical of the match, but most of the feedback over the last couple of days has been very positive. I knew it was going to be a battle of wills instead of a battle of skills. I was fortunate to still be the World Champion when it was all over.

Q: Do you think this match was what you and the NWA needed at this time to showcase the promotion going forward?

A: I think what we needed was a classic NWA style of a match and I think we did that. If I could do it all over again, I'd hit him with my finisher in the middle of the ring and finish him off. If he could do it all over again he would probably tap me out with his finisher, but that's not how the match ended. I think the response from the NWA has been positive. We're on a slow build and that has been the intent from the very beginning. I don't know where this is going, or how it's all going to end, or how long I'll continue to win matches. Every time I win a world title match it's a pleasure and an honor.

Q: What is your response to Billy Corgan's open challenge to your title?

A: I got my third or fourth shot at the NWA World title from Jax Dane, but he didn't have to do that. He had beaten me three other times. I want to be a fighting champion. Anybody that the NWA wants to sanction a match with, I'm 100% behind it. Dane gave me that shot and I'd love to give as many title shots to people as I can.

Q: What has the company told you about their upcoming plans and how do they expect to market the NWA product?

A: Basically, what I and a lot of people have been told is that William Corgan has a 20-year plan. A lot of people say that sounds ridiculous. Sometimes promotions rush things that should take six months, but they are done in 6 weeks. When that happens, that product doesn't always deliver. What William Corgan and Dave Lagana have set out to do is only make commitments that they know that they can follow through on. How many times have we seen a promotion go out with great talent and great funding and be out of money after a few shows? It was because they made commitments that they couldn't keep. That's not going to happen here, because this is going to be a slow roll out. I know for a fact we're ahead of schedule for what they originally predicted and set out to do, so they are very happy with the way that things are going.

Q: How vital is it for the NWA to work with a successful promotion such as Championship Wrestling From Hollywood?

A: William Corgan and Dave Lagana have a plan. It's been said if the NWA doesn't have any affiliates, how can it be the National Wrestling Alliance? They believe that every wrestling organization should be able to work with each other as long as it's mutually beneficial. We are open to working with any wrestling organization as long as the result can be beneficial to both parties. I know there are some things in the works that I can't reveal, but there are some potentially huge things set to happen. The NWA has been reaching out to some organizations, and some other organizations have been reaching out to the NWA. Some of these plans are so big that they rattle my nerves a little bit. We'll see what happens. When Corgan and Lagana know something, I'm sure they will announce it.

Tim Storm vs Americo

Photos by Jon-Paul Le Blanc - 4 Corners Photography

Tim Storm, Lex Luger, & James Beard

BIG RAMP – NOVEMBER 21, 2017

Jon-Paul Le Blanc - 4 Corners Photography

It has been years since iconic legends such as Skandor Akbar, Gary Hart, and Jim Cornette have been orchestrating managerial knowledge outside of the wrestling ring. Today, very few managers exist. An exception to that, is Big Ramp out of New Orleans, Louisiana. He has led the way for Big Ramp Enterprises to be successful for nearly 10 years. Big Ramp has picked up where the wrestling managers of the past have left off.

"Being a manager is a dying art. A lot of the managers today just don't take it serious enough to be innovative and to try new things," Big Ramp said. "The manager's main purpose is to make their client bigger than life. A manager needs to be able to build up and make their client believe in themselves, even when others don't see the best in your client."

Big Ramp's resume speaks for itself. For a decade, his management company has been dominating the wrestling scene all over the United States. Wrestlers such as Monty Warbucks, Barry Wolfe, Rodney Mack, Tyson Dean, and Mustang Mike, are just some of the talents that have been signed by this young and determined entrepreneur. In all, Big Ramp has managed seven world champions, and currently, he manages 75 wrestlers, with 55 of them being various championship title holders throughout the country.

"I help my wrestlers by scanning out their opponents. I scout everybody. We come up with some innovative moves to counter what they do," Big Ramp boasted. "I hate losing. We don't lose, but sometimes, we get a not-win."

Throughout the years, Big Ramp has worked in several wrestling companies including the NWA, Wildkat, Voodoo, Elite, EGO, and Power Slam Pro Wrestling Promotions. The fans that have seen Big Ramp in action are very familiar with his antics. He will do anything to ensure a victory for his clients. Some of the things that Big Ramp has done to his adversaries include throwing fireballs, throwing people through walls, cutting their hair, spray painting them, and he has even dressed up as Santa Claus.

"I love going into my bag of old tricks. A lot of these kids have never seen this stuff before," Big Ramp grinned. "I don't consider myself a good guy or a bad guy. I am probably the worst guy because, in any situation, I'm the last guy that you want to see."

There is a good possibility that you may hear Big Ramp before you see him. That is because he likes to carry around his trusty air horn "Boomquisha." Instead of using it to alert people of his whereabouts, he uses it against the people he does not like. Big Ramps' horn is guaranteed to annoy all in attendance.

"When the fans are not giving my clients the respect that they deserve, I use my air horn to shut them up," Big Ramp said. "I ran it by Jimmy Hart and he thought it was a really good idea."

Having Jimmy Hart approve of Big Ramp's gimmick says a lot. The veteran manager knows something about irritating the audience. Jimmy did it for years with his megaphone. Other managers who have helped shape Big Ramp's career are men like Kevin Sullivan and Paul Heyman.

"They passed along to me some really simple advice that I have found beneficial," Big Ramp responded. "These are people I can call and get some good guidance from when I need it."

With the New Year around the corner, you can expect that Big Ramp is doing everything he can to keep the success that he has created going forward. He is optimistic that his stable of great wrestling talent will continue to grow beyond what the fans could ever imagine.

"We're going to turn it up in 2018. I have a lot of surprises that I plan to unveil," Big Ramp promised. "I have been reaching out to a lot of free agents. We have some really good talent coming to Big Ramp Enterprises."

When it comes to the fans and the opponents that his clients wrestle, Big Ramp is not going to win any popularity contest. What Big Ramp has discovered, however, is a formula that might just secure a place for his name in wrestling history.

"A successful manager is someone who will go all out for their client. Sometimes you even have to put yourself in harm's way," Big Ramp declared. "Sometimes you just have to take a bullet for the team, and not everyone is willing to do that. When you're making an omelet you have to break a couple of eggs."

FUN FACTS
Favorite wrestler: The Missing Link
Career highlight: Managing Rodney Mack & Jax Dane vs Ray Rowe & Lance Hoyt
Favorite band: The Doors
Favorite sports team: New England Patriots
Hobbies: Music, Karate, and community work.
Dog person or cat person: Dog person
A state that you have never been too: Confusion
A movie you have seen multiple times: Pro Wrestlers vs. Zombies
Favorite Actor: Forest Whitaker
Favorite color: Red
A book you have read: Controversy Creates Cash by Eric Bishoff
Favorite dessert: Ice cream

REMEMBERING TUGBOAT TAYLOR
DECEMBER 3, 2017

Wrestleville – Vinny Berry

There have been many tough men in professional wrestling. You can start with some of the easier choices like Terry Funk, Black Jack Mulligan, or Dusty Rhodes, but eventually, the conversation is ultimately going to turn to another wrestler that established his legacy in Texas. That particular wrestler was Tugboat Taylor.

"If you sat down at dinner with him, he was a big Teddy Bear, but if you wronged him, or one of his family members or friends, you knew not to do it again," Tugboat's Son Chaz Taylor shared."Dad was like an enforcer. If anyone in wrestling thought that they were better than the others, he stretched them in the ring and got them back in line."

On November 8th, 2017, at the age of 71, Dick "Tugboat" Taylor passed away. Taylor started his in-ring professional career after being trained by Johnny Valentine in the early '80s. Taylor became a part of Paul Bosch's Houston Wrestling television broadcast, but he also traveled and made his name known in promotions like the NWA, AWA, WWF, World Class, Triple-A, and several others throughout his career.

"It was cool knowing that my dad was a pro wrestler. The kids at school knew who he was because he was on T.V.," Taylor boasted. "He had a reputation for being tough and reliable. If he was booked to be on a show he was always there."

When Chaz was just a baby, his father served as a Marine and was an amateur wrestler who trained the other athletes at Treasure Island on the military squad. It was at that point in Tugboat's amateur career when he had one of his biggest matches. Tugboat suffered a loss that eliminated him from going to the 1972 Olympics in Munich, West Germany.

"He was beating Chris Taylor nine to nothing, but Chris outweighed my dad over a hundred pounds. Dad eventually ran out of steam," Taylor added. "Chris pinned my dad, and he then became the alternate for the team."

After a 26 year career in the pro ranks Tugboat also had his share of competition with elite wrestlers. On any given night, he could be in the ring with guys like Ox Baker, Jerry Blackwell, Bob Orton, and the Junkyard Dog.

"I traveled with him many times and watched him step in the ring with the likes of the Ultimate Warrior, Sting, Ric Flair, Hulk Hogan, and Harley Race," Taylor commented. "It was cool to see him in the ring with the top guys and see him beat the hell out of them. How could a kid not be proud of his father when the crowd was cheering for him? It was a great feeling."

When Tugboat was not in the ring, he was teaching wrestling at his school in Houston, Texas. At his academy, he was known for being a perfectionist and instructing his students to do certain moves until they got them right. He had the opportunity to pass on wrestling to Shawn Hernandez, Stevie Ray, Booker-T, and Ahmed Johnson, just to name a few.

"He showed them how to do something at his gym, and when you watched Dad on tape in his old matches, he did it just like he was teaching his students," Taylor said. "There were a lot of guys that didn't go on to become big names, but a lot of them went out and fulfilled their dreams. Whether they had a lot of money or not, Dad was willing to help them out."

Throughout his lengthy wrestling career, and despite all the traveling, Tugboat was always there for his family when hewasn't out on the road. He not only passed the skill of wrestling on to his son Chaz, but he also taught him several other life lessons.

"If there was a wrestler on the road that was having trouble or was unable to get back home and see his family, my dad always gave him money," Taylor commented. "My dad didn't just train these guys to be pro wrestlers he treated them as if they were his own kids. He went beyond the call of duty, and to me that was impressive. "

DICK TAYLOR
December 9, 1945 – November 8, 2017

Photo by Melissa Woodruff

DJ King with Chaz & Susan Taylor - December 10, 2017

HARLEY RACE – DECEMBER 10, 2017

Photo Courtesy of Harley Race

For three decades Harley Race made his presence known in professional wrestling. The man from Quitman, Missouri may have held his share of titles, but being the National Wrestling Alliance World Heavyweight Champion a total of eight times measures his success. Today, Harley has his World League of Wrestling training school in Troy, Missouri. Wrestling has been a part of his life for 60 years. Harley is very proud of his accomplishments in wrestling. He is grateful he can still pass on the techniques to the new wrestlers coming into the sport.

"I was the greatest wrestler of all time. I was able to perform in the ring the way I did all of those years, no matter who I was in there with," Race stated. "I could do whatever I wanted to do when I wrestled because of my abilities. My opponent knew he was going to get his butt kicked when he got in the ring with me."

Harley was just 13 years old when he went with his father and brother to his very first wrestling match near his hometown. At that moment, Harley fell in love with the sport, and he instantly made a decision that changed his life forever. At that moment he told his family that he was going to become a wrestler.

From the time that Harley was introduced to pro wrestling he could not stop thinking about it. Since he was a minor and still in school his dream job was not an option. At the age of 15, Race came up with a plan that allowed him to train in wrestling on a full-time basis. A plan his parents were not too happy about.

"To make sure I wasn't going to be in school that year I picked a fight with the Principal. I punched him in the mouth and I got kicked out," Race commented. "Once my parents realized that wrestling was what I wanted to do they let me start my training."

By the time Harley was 16 years-old he was in St. Joseph, Missouri, with Gus Karras and his veteran wrestlers. At that time, Karras was putting on wrestling shows there. He was sharing a region that covered a four-state area and co-promoted wrestling matches with Bob Geigle and Pat O'Connor.

"I was wrestling with Gus at some carnivals and in less than a year, I was wrestling on television in St. Jo," Race explained. "Of course at that time he didn't know how old I was and if he did, I wouldn't be doing either one."

With the experience he was gaining from all the different wrestlers he was facing, it allowed him to get good at his game. Harley had the opportunity to wrestle against Pat and that boosted his confidence. Eventually, he got his driver's license which allowed him to start taking matches all over Missouri, Kansas, Iowa, and other areas in the Midwest. It was near Christmas in 1960 when Harley was involved in a serious car accident that claimed the life of his wife. He was severely injured and was out of the sport for a little over a year while his body recovered.

"I have had half a dozen screws in my right knee since then. I also have two braces and 12 pins in my left forearm," Race continued. "The left forearm worked out pretty good because I'm left-handed and after it healed, it worked well with cracking somebody in the jaw with it."

The doctors who treated Harley at the time told him that things were never going to be the same for him. Due to the severity of his injuries and the extent of the surgeries, they did not expect someone in his condition to return to wrestling.

Despite their concerns and recommendations, the accident did not stop Harley. He was determined. Not too long after his return to the ring, he wrestled under Verne Gagne's promotion, the American Wrestling Association. By 1965, he and Larry Hennig dominated the tag team scene and won the AWA World Tag Team Titles when they defeated Dick the Bruiser and The Crusher.

Race and Hennig were very successful and they traveled the world. Unfortunately in 1967, Hennig suffered a knee injury that sidelined him for several months. It was then that Race had the opportunity to show his skills and ability to wrestle well in single matches. He even wrestled against Verne Gagne, the AWA World Heavyweight Champion.

"Verne was very tough. I had a lot of matches with him over the years," Race answered. "His ability and knowledge of wrestling made him very successful."

On May 23rd, 1973, in Kansas City, Missouri, Harley stepped into the ring with the NWA World Heavyweight Champion, Dory Funk Jr. The two men wrestled in a best of two out of three falls match and when it was over, Harley was crowned the champion. It was an accomplishment that was very special to him.

"I got started in the wrestling business because it was something I watched on T.V. and it was something that I truly loved to do," Race added. "To be called the World's Champion at something you love to do, how can it get any better than that?"

It was the beginning of a new era. At that time, the NWA World's Heavyweight Championship was the most prestigious title in wrestling. The NWA was the only promotion recognized for having a worldwide schedule. Wherever the NWA Champion went, he was respected. Being the NWA World Heavyweight Champion had its perks, but it also had a downside. It meant that the title holder stepped in the ring with guys like Jack Brisco, Bobo Brazil, Gene Kiniski, Pat O'Connor, and Terry Funk night after night.

"Being able to go to any territory as a World Champion meant that you were going to be placed in the ring with the very best," Race declared. "I loved doing that."

While Harley was the NWA Champion during the '70s and the '80s, he fought some colorful characters. Dusty Rhodes and Ric Flair were men that he remembers having classic battles with. Rhodes defeated Harley for his coveted belt on August 21st, 1979 in Tampa, Florida, but Rhodes turned it back over to him just 5 days later in a match that lasted nearly 20 minutes in Orlando.

"When I was about to lock up with Dusty, he always said something to make me start laughing," Race grinned. "Dusty was a good wrestler. What he lacked in wrestling, he made up for it on the microphone. We made good money together just about anywhere in the United States."

Wrestling fans who followed the NWA back then know all about the epic matches between Race and Flair. Some of their contests are the best ever. Between January of 1983 and May of 1984, the NWA World Title changed hands four times between the two men. They wrestled each other all over the world in a countless number of matches. The record book says that both men dominated the sport for nearly two years.

"My matches with Ric were some of the toughest that I ever had. Ric was a good wrestler," Race articulated. "He had the ability to move around the ring and do so many different things. He could talk on the microphone and he brought a certain class to wrestling."

__HARLEY RACE__
__April 11, 1943 – August 1, 2019__

BUSHWHACKER LUKE - DECEMBER 21, 2017

Jon-Paul Le Blanc - 4 Corners Photography

As a singles wrestler or in a tag team competition, Luke Williams has made a name for himself. He and his wrestling partner Butch Miller have worked under such names as the Kiwis, the Sheepherders, and the Bushwhackers. However you are familiar with Luke Williams, he has left an impression on the fans.

He solidified his notoriety and became a household name when he wrestled as Bushwhacker Luke in the WWF between 1988 and 1997. His reputation in the ring occurred long before he and Butch decided to work for Vince McMahon.

"The Bushwhacker's run started almost 30 years ago. There are fans that are 30, 35, and 40 years old that don't even know who the Sheepherders were. They've never heard of the Sheepherders," Williams declared. "We were hardcore before hardcore became a name brand."

As the Sheepherders, Williams and Miller were a bit crazed, unstable, and totally unpredictable. They terrorized their opponents and literally scared the fans. Their style was so violent and relentless, that it was not uncommon to see blood when they wrestled. The Sheepherders took part in some of the most dangerous matches ever created.

Their home country of New Zealand has been a long-time ally of the United States, but not to wrestling fans as Williams and Miller flaunted the flag of their motherland and reviled America. The Sheepherders often had an American wrestler accompany them who denounced his country and proudly waved the New

Zealand colors in the middle of the ring for all the fans to see. Their criticism of each state they worked in and their regular usage of the word "Yank" did not help with their popularity.

"We were pit bulls. When it was time for us to take over, we went in and beat up our opponents," Williams responded. "In wrestling, there is a good guy and a bad guy. We were the foreigners and the fans cheered for the hometown boys."

Williams started wrestling in 1962 when he was only 15 years old. In the beginning, it was a hobby for the teenager. At that time, the shows were not as frequent in New Zealand and he wrestled whenever he could. It was in those early days that he met Butch while they were both trained at the local gyms. They did not start wrestling full-time together until 1966.

About that same time, Williams traveled to Australia. Promoter Jim Barnett put on shows in that country. New Zealand wrestlers took on the American talent that Barnett brought there to wrestle. It is possible that Barnett's contribution to wrestling might have helped influence William's future wrestling style.

"Barnett was running shows every day there. He had all of the crazy guys and all of the heavy artillery on his roster," Williams commented. "There is no heavy artillery around anymore. He did the matches with the blood and guts. Jim was a businessman and he wanted to draw money and he did."

By 1972, Williams and Miller made their way to North America and they started wrestling in and around Montreal, Canada as the Kiwis. It was there ,that they met up with Andre the Giant and Killer Kowalski, two wrestlers that they worked with in New Zealand and Australia. The Kiwis wrestled seven days a week. They made a name for themselves in the sport of wrestling, but they were constantly on the move. They ate, went to the gym, traveled to the next town, wrestled, slept, and did it all over again the next day.

"There wasn't much time for pleasure or anything like that. There was no real downtime," Williams added. "We were making money and wrestling was something we liked to do, but it wasn't a party or anything like that. It was work."

Over the next seven years, the Kiwis wrestled in Stampede Wrestling for Stu Hart and then went back to New Zealand for television tapings from time to time. They also wrestled in Europe, Japan, and Hawaii. Their reputation was so unpopular that they were hated and feared everywhere they went. The stay in Hawaii was nice because when the Kiwis were not wrestling, they enjoyed their free time on the beach. The downside, however, was that there wasn't much money to be made in that territory. In 1979, after being there for only a couple of months, they met Roddy Piper who came to the island for a wrestling show. He liked how Williams and Miller worked.

"We told Roddy that we wanted to get out of there so he made a call to Don Owen," Williams recalled. "Shortly thereafter, we were in Northwest Championship Wrestling, and the fans hated us there too."

In Portland Now, they won the territory's tag team belts their first week there as the Sheepherders. They defeated Adrian Adonis and Ron Starr for the belts. Don had plans for his new wrestlers and within six weeks things looked promising. Soon after, a feud broke out between Rick Martel and Piper that series of matches lasted more than a year. As was common in every territory they wrestled in, the Sheepherder's tactics infuriated the fans. The blatant disregard for the rules and their opponent's well being incited negative emotions as far as the audience was concerned.

"We came out of the arenas and our tires were slashed and our windshields were smashed out. That was the kind of heat we had," Williams said. "We learned real quick that we had to start traveling with somebody else."

After their run in the Portland territory, the Sheepherders worked in Memphis and then in San Antonio, Texas. At JoeBlanchard's Southwest Championship Wrestling promotion Williams and Miller sported their signature camouflage pants and tank tops as their in-ring attire. In 1981, Miller left Williams to return to New Zealand to take care of some family matters. Fellow wrestler Jonathan Boyd stepped in to take Miller's place up until 1983.

It was there where Williams gained his experience as a booker. A wrestling booker is someone who recruits and hires talent for the promotion's matches. Williams was responsible for supplying the final television product. From there, Williams took his booking talents to Puerto Rico, a territory where fans had become accustomed to a certain style of wrestling.

"In Puerto Rico we had some different kinds of matches. We had barbed wire matches and fire matches," Williams stated. "It was all blood and guts because the people down there loved that sort of thing."

In 1986, while working for Bill Watts in the Mid-South Wrestling territory, the Sheepherders were involved in one of their most notable feuds. It was against Bobby Fulton and Tommy Rogers, who were known as The Fantastics. The promotion covered a large part of the southeastern region of the United States, including New Orleans, St. Louis, and parts of Texas.

Bobby Fulton and Tommy Rogers were two handsome guys who had muscular bodies to go along with their charming charisma. The Sheepherders were mean and vicious, and loathed by all. There was a big difference between the two teams and it just might have led to the success that fueled this conflict.

"The fans wanted to see them kick our asses," said Williams. "We made them a team that the fans could get behind."

When the rivalry started between the two teams, Watts was putting them in regular tag team match-ups. As the months went on, the four men had all kinds of gimmick matches, until it escalated to them being involved in barbed wire cage matches with each other. Those violent and bloody events went on all over the territory every single day for over a month.

"We knew what we had to give the fans. Those two little guys had big hearts and we drew a lot of money there," Williams declared. "The kids of today wouldn't be doing matches like that. They would be screaming, but today is a whole different era."

In 1988, the Sheepherders had a meeting with Vince McMahon. It was McMahon's idea to turn the duo from some of the most violent wrestlers in the business to good guys. The plan was to create characters that fell between the Moondogs and the

Sheepherders. Moving forward, they were called the Bushwhackers and their personalities changed drastically.

"We told him that we didn't care as long as we had jobs," Williams commented. "In both the NWA and the AWA, you were a wrestler. In the WWF, you were a celebrity. We were making our wrestling pay, but we were also making merchandise money so we were doing pretty well."

When Williams and Miller entered the arena they marched and swung their arms back and forth as they went off to wrestle. They were fun, silly, and adored by the fans. The treatment they received from the audience was nothing like they had experienced before. For wrestling fans who had watched Luke and Butch wrestle in the past, this was something really different from their Sheepherder days. However, the absurd antics did not stop.

"Butch thought we needed to come up with something catchy. He came up with the head licking," Williams chuckled. "The fans stuck their faces out there so we could lick their heads. It was anything but normal."

In 2015, the Bushwhackers were inducted into the WWE Hall of Fame. Some fans did not realize the extent of their wrestling history. Few knew that they once wrestled with the Rock's father and grandfather. Many people were still unaware of their days before they were the Bushwhackers, but after wrestling for five decades, there is not much that Williams and Miller have not seen or done as professional wrestlers.

Today, Williams is 71 years old. He still wrestles and attends wrestling conventions on a regular basis. The events where he can do autograph signings allow him to interact with fans up close and personal. He has met fans that have known him from the different eras of his wrestling career.

"I believe we are still remembered because of the marching and the head licking," Williams grinned. "A fan recently told me, "I liked the Bushwhackers, but my heart was with the Sheepherders. I feared the Sheepherders."

Fear is a common theme when discussing these two wrestlers from New Zealand. The Sheepherder's style was savage and fierce and their work inside the ring is remembered. Williams and Miller knew how to play the villains. In their prime, wrestling was designed that way. Today, wrestling is much different.

"There are no bad guys today. Back then, people bought tickets to see the bad guy get their ass kicked, and that's why the arenas were packed," Williams convinced. "I love the sport and I'm not knocking it, but today it is entertainment just like the circus."

FUN FACTS
Career highlight: #1. One highlight was when I walked into the ring at Wembley Stadium in front of 96,000 people when the Bushwhackers and Jim Duggan took on the Nasty Boys and Mountie. **#2.** A battle royal at Madison Square Garden in the '80s. The last man to enter the match was Hulk Hogan and the crowd went wild. Butch could have talked to me with his mouth right up against my ear and I wouldn't have heard him.

Jon-Paul Le Blanc - 4 Corners Photography

Luke having some words with Brian Thompson - 2014

ALAN STEEL – DECEMBER 30, 2017

Jon-Paul Le Blanc - 4 Corners Photography

If you lived in Memphis, Tennessee during the '70s, '80s, and the '90s, there's a good chance that you watched professional wrestling. For years, that region of the United States was a hotbed for the sport. Wrestlers like Jackie Fargo, Bill Dundee, Jerry Lawler, Austin Idol, and Jimmy Valiant were the reasons why the wrestling scene was on fire there.

Pro wrestler "All That" Alan Steel remembers watching his favorite superstars in the ring. They were such a big part of his life while he was growing up. On most Monday evenings, his father took him to the Mid-South Coliseum so he could watch the matches in person. On Saturday mornings, there was a good chance that Alan was in front of the T.V. watching his favorite show. If by chance he was not at home when wrestling came on, he figured out a way to not miss seeing the weekly program.

"If we were out shopping, I was in the electronics department of the store watching wrestling," Alan Steel said. "My mother always knew where to find me."

In 1997, when Alan was 21 years old he decided that professional wrestling was something he was going to pursue. He met a man named Charlie Parks. Parks ran an outlaw promotion in the area who agreed to train Alan. Around that same time, Alan also met Sid Vicious. Vicious agreed to train him as well. As it turned out, both men never followed through with his training, so

Alan decided to try something else.

"I wrote Channel 5 a letter and asked if the local promotion which was Power Pro Wrestling had a wrestling school," Steel said. "A week later, I received a letter back from the station and they gave me Bill Dundee's phone number."

A few weeks after making contact with Bill Dundee, Alan found himself traveling from Memphis to McKenzie, Tennessee every Wednesday night. There he was taught the in-ring sport from Bill and his son Jamie. Alan learned the fundamentals of wrestling. He was also educated on the psychology of wrestling, which is not just how to do something, but when you do it and why.

"You're never going to see Bill teach anybody how to do a moonsault or anything that is not of the old school style," Steel interjected. "When it came to wrestling I was taught that if I didn't believe in it, then nobody else believed in it either."

Alan trained for six months and he also worked as a referee before he stepped into the ring to wrestle in his first match. Throughout his training period, some of the sessions were intense and repetitious. Dundee stressed to him the importance of paying attention to the details. Now, 20 years later, Alan is still wrestling and everything that Bill passed on to him has served him well. From time to time throughout his career, he has wrestled with the WWE and has done some extra work for them as well.

"It was disappointing not to get called up by the WWE, but I've known from day one that you can be one of the most talented guys out there and still not get a job," Steel sighed. "The WWE looks at thousands of guys every year and only a handful of them get signed. You got to have the "IT factor," and that depends on who's looking at you what determines the "IT factor" in my opinion."

In 1998, Alan had the opportunity to be on television with Power Pro Wrestling his first year in the business. Things went well for him until the promotion's owners made a business deal with Vince McMahon and Power Pro Wrestling ultimately turned into a developmental system for the WWF. With the WWF's talent coming in, most of the wrestlers that were there before the merger got pushed to the side, and Alan was one of them.

Some of the wrestlers that came to Power Pro Wrestling under contract with the WWF at that time were guys like Kurt Angle, Prince Albert, Rikishi, Crash Holly, Brian Kendrick, and Daniel Bryan. When they were in Memphis most of them wrestled under different names from what they are known as today. Those were the people Alan was wrestling with. The changes that took place at Power Pro Wrestling were discouraging for Alan and his fellow wrestlers. However, the opportunity also served as a positive experience for them because of all the different styles and influences the new wrestlers brought with them.

"If you didn't learn anything, it was your fault because we were put in this melting pot of talent. It was an amazing time!" Steel exclaimed. "I took advantage of the opportunity to show everyone that I could hang with the guys, and I was hoping to be noticed by the individuals handing out contracts for the WWF."

Even though things did not turn out the way that Alan had hoped for, he still credits that period of his wrestling career to the most fun that he has ever had. Alan has a love and appreciation for wrestling that goes further than just the ring. It transcends to the audience and the locker room as well. For Alan, the journey has been "All that." Few wrestlers can say that they have been able to continue in the sport for as long as Alan has. He was planning to retire at the age of 40, but at 41 he is still going at it. The wrestling dates are not as plentiful as they once were, but he does have certain promotions in Tennessee, Mississippi, and Arkansas that he likes to work with.

"I've never done drugs in my life, but if I had a drug of choice it would be pro wrestling. I get my fix almost every weekend," Steel grinned. "Some people are born to wrestle, and I feel that I'm one of those people."

FUN FACTS
Favorite wrestler: "Mr. Perfect" Curt Hennig
Favorite sports team: The San Francisco 49ers during the Joe Montana & Steve Young era.
Hobbies: Weightlifting, playing video games, and watching movies with my wife.
Dog person or a cat person: A dog person
A state that I've never been to Washington
Favorite food: Pizza
A movie I've seen multiple times: I-Robot
Favorite actor: Tom Cruise
Favorite color: Gray
A book I have read: Hulk Hogan's biography
Favorite dessert: Banana pudding

Jon-Paul Le Blanc - 4 Corners Photography

Bill Dundee & Alan Steel - 2015

CW ANDERSON – JANUARY 19, 2018

Jon-Paul Le Blanc - 4 Corners Photography

Stars, thunderous bangs, and bright flashes of light are the details that describe a stormy night sky, but for wrestlers like CW Anderson it might just sound like Extreme Championship Wrestling. The 47-year-old wrestler from Raleigh, North Carolina has been wrestling for 24 years. When he walks through the curtain to the ring, he wants to prove only one thing.

"That CW Anderson is the baddest man on the planet. I don't care who you are in the ring, you are not going to beat me," CW Anderson said. "I tell the kids I wrestle with today that you might be a better athlete than me, but you are not going to outwork me. I'm smart, I know how to get the point across, and I want the fans to love the babyface by hating me so much."

Work ethic has always been important to CW. That principal was instilled in him from the time he was a young child. Growing up on a farm, he learned the discipline of hard work by putting in long hours on his family's property when he was not in school.

"I grew up in the country so I was outside feeding the animals, slaughtering hogs, farming, or whatever it was. I worked a lot while growing up," Anderson mentioned. "On the weekends, if I wasn't barning tobacco for my grandfather, I was barning tobacco for other people. I didn't mind working."

Some fans might find it hard to believe, but there was a time that CW was not interested in the pro wrestling. It was his brother that was the big wrestling fan in their house. One day, CW's brother talked him into sitting down and watching it with him. The match that was on television was Ivan Koloff and Krusher Kruschev defending their NWA tag team titles against the Rock n' Roll Express.

"The Rock n' Roll Express won by Ricky rolling up Uncle Ivan for the pin," Anderson recalled. "I specifically remember running and jumping around the room screaming that the Rock n' Roll Express had just defeated the Russians. That got me hooked."

Baseball was the game that CW had a passion for and it was something he was very good at. CW played catcher in high school where he caught the attention of college and pro scouts by being able to throw the ball to second base at 90 miles an hour from his knees. One of the teams that were interested in CW was the San Diego Padres. His mother encouraged him to go to college to further his education so he studied to be a video game designer. While he was playing baseball at Columbus State Community College, he hyper extended his arm.

"I was showing off and I tried to pick somebody off at the first base by throwing from my knees," Anderson added. "I came home and my baseball career never went anywhere after that. Since then, my arm has never really been the same."

Back at home in 1993 while waiting in line at a McDonalds', CW ran into a buddy that he had not seen for quite some time. The two men talked about what they were doing and CW found out that his friend was doing some independent wrestling. The friend invited him to come to a show and CW accepted the offer.

"I showed up early and got in the ring with him. We started messing around and rolling around. I kind of got hooked and I haven't left the ring since," Anderson commented. "It was then when I thought that this was something that I could do. I have the type of personality that if I am going to do something, I'm going to be the best at it."

CW made his professional debut on December 4th, 1993, and from there he cut his teeth on the independent wrestling circuit. The one thing he did differently than most wrestlers throughout his career was he kept a full-time job. His big break on national television came in 1999 when he started wrestling for Extreme Championship Wrestling.

If you have ever seen Extreme Championship Wrestling, you might remember it for the hardcore style that it presented. There was violence, risk-taking moves, barbed wire, tables, and of course, let's not forget the use of the chairs. ECW captivated the audience and elevated a large amount of its roster to superstar status.

"Just because it was called Extreme it didn't mean that there was going to be chair shots and blood every night," Anderson affirmed. "Being able to wrestle in front of that crowd was an intense experience because you had to bring you're A-game every night."

CW and his counterparts pushed each other to succeed and they all wanted to see the best from each other. Although the wrestling they were doing was very physical, they hated to see when their friends got hurt. Because of the intense reputation that ECW had, not everybody walked away injury-free. CW experienced at least 17 concussions when he wrestled there and that is because the metal chairs they were using to hit each other with were real.

"Your body is not designed to take chair shots like that. People thought the chairs were fake, but they aren't" Anderson insisted. "A lot of times, adrenaline got me through a match because I didn't drink or do drugs. It was pure adrenaline because the hardest thing I ever took was an aspirin."

In the year and a half that CW spent with the ECW promotion he had some great matches. Some of those opponents were New Jack, Kid Kash, 2 Cold Scorpio, Balls Mahoney, and several others. One match that stands in a class all by itself is the "I Quit Match" he had with Tommy Dreamer in 2001. The two men started attacking each other as they were introduced to the crowd and before you knew it, the fight quickly made its way to the outside of the ring. The ring posts, the guardrails, and the cement flooring all became dangerous available weapons.

"The suplex on the floor was extremely painful," Anderson recalled. "Tommy told me before the match that if it was good, he'd shake my hand when it was over."

The contest was physical and intense. Both Dreamer and Anderson were relentless in their attack and there were times when the fans thought they were going to kill each other. Each man was determined to finish off the other as they traded back and forth with merciless submission holds. If the match was not exciting enough, the interference from the promotion's towel boy, the use of metal cooking sheets, steel chairs, and razor wire helped set the tone for a spectacle that no one could take their eyes off of.

"We were going to do barbed wire across my face, but we couldn't find any. We found some razor wire and Tommy said I could suplex him on it because I wasn't going to put that across my face," Anderson said. "I think we could have taken it a little too far with some stuff, but I really think it was just right."

In the end, Tommy made CW relent. The weapon that he used was a long strip of vinyl trim from a broken table. Tommy used it to pull CW's neck back while he lay on his stomach in the middle of the ring. In all, the match was right under 15 minutes and the fans gave both men a standing ovation for their efforts. Ultimately, Tommy shook CW's hand after the match.

"It's hard to explain how we got it right," Anderson continued. "We must have got something right because fans are still talking about it 17 years later."

To have that kind of a match with Tommy Dreamer would be important to anyone's career. At the time, Tommy was the face of ECW and he had a reputation for going all out. Tommy is known for giving a hundred percent of his effort inside the ring.

"He always pushed me to be better. Tommy always knew I had it in me to be one of the top guys there," Anderson reassured. "So when I was in the ring with him, I always wanted to prove to him that I deserved to be there."

Today, on almost any weekend, you can still find CW wrestling on the independent scene. The sport is still fun for him. He still enjoys entertaining the fans and being around the boys. Because he has a strong passion and high regard for the business, what he has done throughout his career is important to him.

"I hope that the fans feel like they always got their money's worth, and I hope they knew I always gave a hundred percent," Anderson replied. "As long as I can still do that, I am going to keep on wrestling."

FUN FACTS
Favorite Wrestle: Bobby Eaton
Career Highlight: My "I quit match" with Tommy Dreamer.
Favorite band: Lincoln Park
Hobbies: Playing video games, playing chess and collecting chess sets.
Dog or cat person: Both, but right now I have six dogs.
A movie that you have seen multiple times: Gladiator
Favorite Actor: Denzel Washington & Tom Hanks
A book you've read: Da Vinci Code

SHEA SUMMERS - FEBRUARY 11, 2018

Jon-Paul Le Blanc - 4 Corners Photography

Shea Summers may only be 19 years old, but she is making a huge impact on the independent wrestling scene. The wrestler who bears the nickname of the Thunder Blonde with her black leather jacket and her edgy attitude are reminiscent of her days as a punk rocker. Her presence in the ring is leaving an impression on wrestling fans in the south-east region of the United States.

"Showmanship has always been a part of me and I think that's why I like wrestling. It gives me a stage where I can perform and there's so much that goes into it," Shea Summers said. "What I used to do in theater or in my band didn't feel like it was enough. The showmanship that I have within myself connects with everything I do in wrestling."

Shea grew up near Atlanta, Georgia, where all of her family lived. By the time she was in the 6th grade she moved to Pensacola, Florida. The move was difficult for Shea and she had trouble accepting the change. She had her good days and her bad days, but the in-ring sport of wrestling was always there for her.

"I've watched wrestling since I was a little kid and I really can't tell you what drew me to it. I think watching wrestling took me away from negative things and as I got older, I felt like I had to do it," Summers commented. "You have to admit it's kind of a weird thing to like. It seems to be an outcast sport that not everybody is into."

There were many wrestlers that Shea enjoyed watching back in the day. One of the women wrestlers that left an impression on her was Jazz. Some might know Jazz from her stint in ECW where she competed against men. Others will remember her as being WWE's and NWA's Women's World Champion, but many cannot forget the epic battles that she had with Trish Stratus in the early 2000s.

"I really like Jazz because she's a powerhouse and really cool," Summers added. "A lot of women back then didn't get a lot of chances, but she was one of the ones who actually did."

Shea started training in June of last year and broke out on the independent scene in October. Since then, Shea has been on the road and wrestling on as many shows that she can get herself booked on. She has been working with promotions in Florida, Mississippi, Georgia, and Louisiana.

"What I've found out is that you really don't stop learning. Especially when you haven't been wrestling for very long," Summers said. "Right now, I'm training and I'm going to a lot of seminars. I'm willing to wrestle anywhere because I want to learn as much as I can and as fast as I can."

Shea had the opportunity to attend a wrestling seminar this past December at the Power Factory in Atlanta. Several wrestlers from the Monster Factory in New Jersey were there, along with other well-established wrestlers in the business. Some of the pros that participated in training sessions at the seminar were Christopher Daniels, Punishment Martinez, Glacier, QT Marshall, and Daffney.

"It felt like everybody at the seminar had a new way of thinking. I was trained with the influences of a traditional old-school style," Summers replied. "I took notes and I was writing down everything that they were saying to us."

One of the trainers that Shea connected with at the seminar was Daffney. Daffney made her debut in 1999 with WCW.She gained the attention of wrestling fans around the world with the help of television exposure. Throughout her nearly 20 year career in wrestling, Daffney has wrestled, acted as a manager, and has even served as a referee, which has allowed her to gain a wealth of knowledge of the sport. Having all of that knowledge makes her an asset for anyone who wants to break into professional wrestling.

"It was really cool to talk to and be trained by someone who was on T.V. She opened my eyes to a lot of things and put an emphasis on the details," Summers continued. "She stressed that when you are in the ring, showmanship is everything. It was an honor to be taught by her."

Shea has been in professional wrestling a short period of time and to most veterans, she is considered green. The main components that this girl from Georgia has, is heart, determination, and a brain for the business. Her open mind and willingness to put in all the necessary work to be successful is endless. Talk to her for a few minutes and you can tell she is ahead of the game in so many ways.

"I have learned that wrestling is about paying your dues and earning your spot," Summers answered. "It is also important to respect the veterans in the business. To some that isn't very important, but it should be for everyone in wrestling."

Shea loves wrestling and she wants to do it as much as possible. This year she is hoping to continue wrestling throughout the southern region of the United States, especially in Florida. She also wants to make her wrestling debut in Texas. For Shea, wrestling goes beyond the ring. It is her passion and it's in her blood.

"I really appreciate this business and it's something I have always wanted to do," Summers stated. "I want to share my stories in the ring and I want people to enjoy my matches."

Shea does come with a guarantee. After her opponents have squared off with her inside the ring, they will know what it's like to roll with the Thunder!

DROP DEAD DALE WYLDE – MARCH 4, 2018

Jon-Paul Le Blanc - 4 Corners Photography

For the past five years, the Pro Wrestling Mid-South promotion based out of Dyersburg, Tennessee has been dominated by one man. That man is the Golden Boy, none other than Greg Anthony. On December 9th of last year, all of that changed when Drop Dead Dale Wylde defeated Greg to win the Unified Heavyweight Championship at the Herb Welch Wrestleplex. The 24-year-old wrestler who hails from Climax, Michigan, is not only known for his in-ring abilities, but also his attire and accessories. Regularly Wylde can be seen with a mirror in hand and he is determined to bring the zebra print pattern back into fashion.

"When Greg says that he is pound for pound and inch per inch the best in professional wrestling, he's not lying," Dale Wylde said. "We've crossed paths several times in my short career and that was the first time I pinned his shoulders to the mat. That was a big win for me"

Since being Champion, Dale has already given Greg four rematches for the title that he himself has held a record seven times. Dale believes that he has been more than accommodating to the Golden Boy as far as giving him the opportunity to win his belt back.

"He has more than overstayed his welcome and he no longer has the opportunity to regain the title as long as I am Champion," Wylde declared. "I think his time on top has run its course. Pro Wrestling Mid South needs a fresh face to carry the banner. I'm more than capable to take this promotion to new heights."

2016 was a great year for Dale. He teamed up with Van Van Horne and the two men achieved great success in tag-team competition as the Love Connection. Not only did they hold the Pro Wrestling Mid South Tag Titles on two different occasions, but they were also voted tag team of the year.

"We meshed together very well. He has a good brain for wrestling with all of the years of experience he has behind him," Wylde replied. "He was able to teach me a thing or two with all his knowledge, but the thing that held me back was that I had to depend on a person that was not "Drop Dead.""

In October of that same year, Wylde and Van Horne had an opportunity to challenge Rob Conway and Matt Riviera for the NWA World Tag Team titles. Unfortunately, their shot at gold did not pan out as they came up short in their effort. That loss stirred up some bitter emotions between The Love Connection.

"It's a story that is told all too often. Van got pinned again. After it happens so many times, that becomes a problem," Wylde affirmed. "It's okay to forgive yourself for your own mistakes, but it's a lot harder to forgive others when they're costing you."

With the love between Van Horne and Wylde fading away, their once successful partnership was on the rocks. 2017 was a year of rebuilding for Dale. It gave him a chance to take a good long look in the mirror, which is easy to do since he is "Drop Dead."

Despite the disappointments he faced with his now former partner Van Horne, in July Dale stepped into the ring with then NWA World Heavyweight Champion Tim Storm. For Dale, wrestling for the NWA World Title is something that many wrestlers never get a shot at, especially since he has only been in the sport a short time. The match lasted almost 20 minutes, and ended by pin fall when Storm caught Dale in his signature move the Perfect Storm.

"Although I was on the losing end of that championship match, I know the outcome will be very different if I get the opportunity again," Wylde stated. "At the time of our match my head was kind of diluted because I was too busy slapping hands and kissing babies. Not having a intense focus held me back in that match."

Dale is showing more focus with an edgier attitude now. He wears his new Pro Wrestling Mid South Unified Heavyweight Championship belt with pride. Dale knows that wrestlers are lining up to take it from him. Men like Josh Mathews, Koko Anderson, and Meklakov the Russian Wrecking Ball are challenging him regularly. Although all those combatants are worthy contenders, Dale has a message for them.

"Lace your boots up tight and bring a lunch. At 24 years of age, I have full confidence in saying that I am one of the smartest wrestlers around. I'm one of the best to step inside that squared circle," Wylde boasted. "I have held multiple championship titles. I was rookie of the year, part of the tag team of the year, and I'm well on the way to being 2018's wrestler of the year."

Jon-Paul Le Blanc - 4 Corners Photography

Dale Wylde in 2018

BRUCE THARPE – MARCH 18, 2018

Jon-Paul Le Blanc - 4 Corners Photography

In 2012, Bruce Tharpe, a South Texas Attorney, acquired the National Wrestling Alliance. Tharpe's passion for wrestling and his understanding of the historic tradition that the NWA once had motivated him to preserve and elevate the company's marketing brand. In 2017, Tharpe sold the 70-year-old promotion to Smashing Pumpkin's front man, Billy Corgan. Wrestleville spoke to Tharpe about the NWA's history, what he accomplished while being President & CEO there, why he sold the promotion, and what his hopes are for the new ownership.

Q: What do you think the NWA and its history mean to the sport of wrestling?

A: The NWA World Championship dates back to the days of Lou Thesz, Ed "The Strangler" Lewis, George Hackenschmidt, Frank Gotch, and those types of guys. There is no other championship in wrestling that has that kind of history.

Q: Do you think the wrestlers of today understand the allure that the NWA promotion once had?

A: It really depends on the wrestler. Over the past few years, I have met many different wrestlers around the world and on the road. Some of them have a lot of respect for the history and the traditions of professional wrestling. Other wrestlers that I have met don't care for anything in the past. They look through the windshield and not the rear view mirror. They don't care about psychology or learning about how things were done. It really depends on the wrestler and where they are at personally.

Q: What made you want to sell the NWA?

A: I took the NWA about as far as I could. Then, along came Billy Corgan and we had extensive meetings with each other. I felt like if I was going to pass the torch, he'd be the best guy to pass it along to. Billy expressed great admiration for the brand, its history, and the tradition of the NWA that I share. Billy has connections in the entertainment industry and he also has the money. It was bittersweet to turn the brand over to somebody else, but I think Billy will be able to take the brand to the next level. I believe he can get the NWA on national television once again.

Q: What was your proudest accomplishment while you were the owner of the NWA?

A: I feel like I successfully negotiated a contractual agreement with New Japan Pro Wrestling and we traveled to Japan 18 times in four years. We appeared on multiple worldwide pay-per-views. The pinnacle for me was appearing at the Tokyo Dome in front of 35,000 people and being in the corner of then NWA World Heavyweight Champion Rob Conway. I think that was the last public appearance of Harley Race, and during that match, he actually knocked me out of the ring. It definitely hurt, but the memories that went along with that will last for the rest of my life. Pain is temporary, but pride is forever.

Q: While you were the NWA President & CEO, was there something that you wanted to accomplish that you were not able to do?

A: My main goal was to get the National Wrestling Alliance back on television and I was not able to accomplish that. Wrestling is a tough sell. People these days are watching reality television. People's attention spans are a lot shorter and you have to produce your television programs in such a way that prevent them from changing the channel. People are always looking for something different. Television executives are making more money these days with different types of television programming other than wrestling. If you're a television production company and all you have is wrestling to sell, it's difficult, because you've got all your eggs in one basket. Big television programmers are looking for something different than the same model that they've seen for the last 20 years.

Q: What are your hopes for Billy Corgan and moving forward with the company?

A: I hope he can get the product on national television and he continues to develop the brand. In the same positive way that he's been doing in the last eight or 10 months.

Q: What do you think Billy has to do to make the NWA successful once again?

A: That is really a question you need to direct to Mr. Corgan. I say that for this reason. He's got his own business plan and he's got his own ideas. He's been very successful in the music industry so as an entrepreneur, he's going to apply those same ideas to the wrestling profession. Billy has a very talented partner in David Lagana who is a well-experienced television producer. So in terms of what they have to do to make the company more successful, that is really a question you'll need to direct to them. I know that Billy has a lot of good ideas and far be it from me to give him any ideas on where to take the company in the future.

Jon-Paul Le Blanc - 4 Corners Photography

Bruce Tharpe with Doc Gallows in 2015

SIR MO – APRIL 19, 2018

Photo by Bobby Horne

Sir Mo & Mable

Before Bobby Horne wrestled in the WWF as Mo with the tag team Men on a Mission, his life already had a purpose with a special calling. However, back then, he might not have known about it. Today, Bobby is 51 years old, and the trainer at Bumps and Bruises Pro Wrestling Academy. He is also the matchmaker for SOAR Championship Wrestling. He takes a powerful anti-bullying message to schools in the Dallas area, and he uses professional wrestling to steer kids away from going down a negative path in their lives.

"People want to feel loved. They want to feel wanted and they don't want to be treated as an outcast," Bobby Horne said. "My whole goal before I die is to save one million kids, and that will be through the process of me saving one, and that person saving one, and so on."

Growing up in North Carolina, Bobby's father was not always in the picture so he looked up to his older brother Gerald. Bobby was denied the discipline, guidance, and love that came from having a father present in his everyday life. By the time he was 10, he had gotten into some trouble when he broke into a store. Now with a juvenile record, Bobby was put on probation for three years. That incident was a wake-up call for him and he straightened up. The ordeal shaped how he continued with his life going forward.

"I needed a father or a good role model," Horne replied. "So, I decided that I'd be a father to any kid who needed or wanted one."

In 1988, Bobby was medically discharged from the United States Army. Two years later, he worked at a rent-to-own store and was also a Sunday school teacher. However, he missed the brotherhood that he experienced in the service and thought there was something more that he could be doing with his life. One day, he went to an independent wrestling show in Charlotte and was impressed with what he saw. After the matches, Bobby approached Gene Anderson, an original member of the Minnesota Wrecking Crew. Bobby asked Gene how he could get into the sport.

A week later, Bobby showed up at Gene's wrestling school in Monroe, North Carolina with $300.00 that Gene had asked for. Bobby thought he was going there for a tryout or to show Gene what he was able to do, but it turned out more like a weeding out process. For nearly five hours Gene tortured him. That day Bobby did 3,000 squats, ran more than 15 miles, and performed the countless amounts of push-ups and wind sprints. On top of all that, he executed multiple firemen carries, in which he ran 50 yards at a time with someone on his back.

"He damn near ran me to death. When it was over, my friends had to pick me up and put me in the car and carry me home," Horne admitted. "I had complete muscle failure, but I didn't quit, and because of that, Gene agreed to train me."

Bobby was into his second week of training when he met 19-year-old Nelson Frazier. Nelson was from Goldsboro, North Carolina and he came to Charlotte to see if he could also be trained in professional wrestling. The teenager was six feet and ten inches tall and weighed 560 pounds. He was constantly getting into trouble. Nelson was accompanied by his father, who was concerned for his well-being. Bobby had a chance to talk to the young man's dad.

"He asked me if I could help keep Nelson out of trouble," Horne commented. "I felt honored, and I took his request very serious. I wanted to fulfill his wishes."

Nelson also made it through his wrestling tryout. Bobby invited Nelson to move into his apartment so he did not have to travel so far for his wrestling training. At that time, Butch Reed and Ron Simmons were wrestling as a tag team in WCW. On Nelson's second day of training, he and Bobby decided to create a tag team of their own.

"Our total combined weight was over 850 pounds. If you go back and look at some of our earlier matches, we didn't work in the ring like we were big or out of shape," Horne responded. "We were big guys but moved well inside the ring. That stood out to everybody. We were very agile for our size."

When the men finished their training they wrestled for the Pro Wrestling Federation, an independent promotion run by George South and Gary Sabaugh. They put on wrestling shows throughout the Carolinas and in Virginia. Bobby and Nelson wrestled as the Knight Brothers and they called themselves the Harlem Knights. George became their mentor and he taught the two men how to polish up their in-ring skills. The downside was that the two men were not getting paid to wrestle. George encouraged them to seek out wrestling opportunities in Memphis. George was familiar with the USWA promotion and thought Bobby and Nelson could do well there.

In April of 1993, after two years of working with George, Bobby and Nelson decided to drive to Memphis. They took their last 40 dollars with them and drove 14 hours to meet the owners of the USWA wrestling promotion, Jerry and Jeff Jarrett. The tag team brought photos of themselves and videotaped matches to show the Jarrett's. Bobby and Nelson slept in their car at the TV 5 Studio so they could catch Jeff and Jerry when they showed up for work on Saturday morning. The Jarrett's were so impressed by the size of the Harlem Knights that they had them do promo interviews that morning. The next day, the two men went to Jonesboro, Arkansas for a tryout and they were hired that night. On the following evening Bobby and Nelson wrestled Jerry Lawler and Jeff Jarrett in the main event at the Mid-South Coliseum in front of 8,000 people.

"We were there three days and they put us in the main event. We got paid 150 bucks a piece that night," Horne grinned. "For two guys who worked as long as we did without ever getting paid, to us, we felt like we had made it."

They wrestled all the top names in the USWA. As the summer season approached the Jarrett's needed to downsize and unfortunately, they started with the Harlem Knights. It was a disappointing time for the two friends because they moved to Memphis just to wrestle. Fellow wrestler Brian Christopher informed Jerry Jarrett of Bobby and Nelson's decision to come to the USWA. Jerry told them that he would make some phone calls. He was confident that he could get the Harlem Knights a tryout with the WWF, or a job with the WCW by the following Monday. When Monday morning came the phone rang before Bobby ever got out of bed.

"It was J.J. Dillon, and he said that Jerry Jarrett had arranged a tryout for us. They flew us out to Portland, Maine the next day. They pretty much hired us on the spot and we really couldn't believe it was happening," Horne explained. "It seemed like we were always getting put in these situations that worked out better than if we stayed doing what we were doing."

Bobby and Nelson teamed up with Greg Girard who became their rapping manager. Bobby was called Mo, Greg went by Oscar, and Nelson's name would be Mable. Together they were known as the Men on a Mission. Bobby and Nelson went all over the world with the WWF, but they also wrestled against the best stars in the business. On any given night, they were stepping into the ring with the likes of Shawn Michaels and Kevin Nash, the Headshrinkers, the Smoking Gunns, or the Quebecers.

"Working with the Quebecers was like having a night off. Jacques Rougeau was brilliant and he knew how to bring the best out of us," Horne stated. "When you're on the Indie scene, you're not learning something new each night because you're working with people you can't learn from. Most of the time, you're working with people that you're trying to teach."

Men on a Mission had a three-year run in the WWF that lasted between 1993 and 1996. Some of the team's highlights included becoming the WWF World Tag Team Champions, appearing at Wrestlemania 10, and Mable winning the King of the Ring tournament.

"Nelson was an amateur wrestler in high school and he always wanted to be in the WWF," Horne said. "It wasn't my dream, but Nelson talked about it so much that I wanted to see if we could do it and we did."

It was not just about wrestling in the WWF for Bobby and Nelson. Additionally, Vince McMahon had them on a mission. The two wrestlers visited inner-city youth programs and community centers and shared positive message of hope with the children. Since the wrestlers knew exactly what the children had to deal with they connected with them right away.

Helping young people escape from hopeless situations did not start for Bobby with Men on a Mission. It started long before that. It started in North Carolina when he met Nelson at Gene Anderson's wrestling school and where he ultimately made a promise to Nelson's dad. On February 18, 2014, Nelson died of a heart attack. His death hit Bobby hard. For six years, the two friends lived together and achieved out their wrestling dreams together. Bobby and Nelson remained close friends for 24 years.

"We didn't have any animosity between each other, and we loved each other. I couldn't have asked for a better tag team partner," Horne affirmed. "Nelson was top-notch. He was like my big little brother."

Photo Courtesy of Bobby Horne

Bobby talking at a school

BARBIE HAYDEN

Jon-Paul Le Blanc - 4 Corners Photography

NWA WORLD WOMEN'S CHAMPION
January 25, 2014 - February 7, 2015

PAUL LEE vs. TOKYO MONSTER KAHAGAS
JULY 12, 2014

Jon-Paul Le Blanc - 4 Corners Photography

Paul Lee

Tokyo Monster Kahagas

Lee in trouble

Lee attempting a toe spin

Lee vs. Tokyo

Tokyo going for the pin

THE VON ERICHS - NOVEMBER 1, 2014
Jon-Paul Le Blanc - 4 Corners Photography

Marshall

Kevin

Ross

Kevin with a yellow rose

Ross & Marshall

Kevin & Tim Brooks

The Von Erichs in victory

SHAWN HERNANDEZ & MICHAEL FAITH
vs.
LA PARK & EL HIJO DE LA PARK
JULY 14, 2017
Wrestleville - Vinny Berry

Shawn Hernandez & Michael Faith

La Park & El Hijo De La Park

Michael vs. La Park

El Hijo diving onto Shawn

El Hijo in mid-air

Shawn attempting to pin La Park

ROB LOVE vs. BRYSIN SCOTT
NOVEMBER 19, 2017
Jon-Paul Le Blanc - 4 Corners Photography

Brysin Scott

Prince Travion

Rob Love

Brysin fighting back

Rob stomping on Brysin

Rob with a headlock on Brysin

Brysin twisting Rob's arm

SUPER TEX BRENT McKENZIE

Jon-Paul Le Blanc - 4 Corners Photography

Brent McKenzie

Brent, Ken Johnson, & Moonshine Mantell

Tony Brooklyn and Brent having a word

Hambone Lee vs. Brent

Brent in all his glory

Ray Rowe vs. Brent McKenzie

195

BIG RAMP ENTERPRISES
Jon-Paul Le Blanc - 4 Corners Photography

BIG RAMP

ALABAMA WRESTLING FEDERATION

Jon-Paul Le Blanc - 4 Corners Photography

SHOOTER JACKSON

ALABAMA WRESTLING FEDERATION
Jon-Paul Le Blanc - 4 Corners Photography

DIAMOND ROBERTS

BATTLEZONE MISSISSIPPI

Jon-Paul Le Blanc - 4 Corners Photography

BRAXTON HUNTER

BATTLEZONE MISSISSIPPI

Jon-Paul Le Blanc - 4 Corners Photography

NIGHTMARE JERIMIAH

BAYOU INDEPENDENT PRO WRESTLING

Jon-Paul Le Blanc - 4 Corners Photography

ADAM ASHER

BAYOU INDEPENDENT PRO WRESTLING
Jon-Paul Le Blanc - 4 Corners Photography

KALEB KONNLEY

DIAMOND CHAMPIONSHIP WRESTLING
Jon-Paul Le Blanc- 4 Corners Photography

BRYMSTONE

DIAMOND CHAMPIONSHIP WRESTLING

Jon-Paul Le Blanc- 4 Corners Photography

MAC DADDY DUDS

GULF STATE WRESTLING

Jon-Paul Le Blanc - 4 Corners Photography

ANDREW ANDERSON

GULF STATE WRESTLING

Jon-Paul Le Blanc - 4 Corners Photography

JORDAN JAA

HOODMARK LUCHA LIBRE

Jon-Paul Le Blanc - 4 Corners Photography

ROCKELLE VAUGHN & BIG RAMP

HOODMARK LUCHA LIBRE

Jon-Paul Le Blanc - 4 Corners Photograph

RICKY REYES

LOKO WRESTLING

Jon-Paul Le Blanc - 4 Corners Photography

GINO MEDINA

LOKO WRESTLING

Jon-Paul Le Blanc - 4 Corners Photography

LADY DIAMOND

PREMIER HOUSTON

Jon-Paul Le Blanc - 4 Corners Photography

BABY BOY

PREMIER HOUSTON

Jon-Paul Le Blanc - 4 Corners Photography

ROTTWIELER JAY DAVIS

PRO WRESTLING 225

Jon-Paul Le Blanc - 4 Corners Photography

XTIAN BLAKE

PRO WRESTLING 225

Jon-Paul Le Blanc - 4 Corners Photography

Wild Thing Michael Boudreaux

SOUTHERN CHAMPIONSHIP WRESTLING

Jon-Paul Le Blanc - 4 Corners Photography

SKYLER

SOUTHERN CHAMPIONSHIP WRESTLING
Jon-Paul Le Blanc - 4 Corners Photography

VLADIMIR KOLOFF

SOUTHWEST WRESTLING ENTERTAINMENT
Jon-Paul Le Blanc - 4 Corners Photography

CHANDLER HOPKINS

SOUTHWEST WRESTLING ENTERTAINMENT
Jon-Paul Le Blanc - 4 Corners Photography

JAZZ

SOUTHWEST WRESTLING ENTERTAINMENT
Jon-Paul Le Blanc - 4 Corners Photography

MIRANDA GORDY

SOUTHWEST WRESTLING ENTERTAINMENT
Jon-Paul Le Blanc - 4 Corners Photography

T-RAY WATFORD

SPECIAL THANKS

I want to thank my wife Sandy Berry for her patience and understanding during this project. Without her support this book would not have been possible. Thank you for believing in me! I love you!

Cover & Graphics – Iron Skull Productions.

Layouts – Wrestleville

Photography – Jon-Paul Le Blanc & 4 Corners Photography

Editors & Proof Readers – David Parker, Gary Klier, Cole Denckla, & Diane Freeland

Advice, Guidance & Support – Jeff Bonugli, John Cannon, Kenny Casanova, Scott Coyer, Chris Inoferio, Rex Leach, Jenny Martinez, Raul Ramos, Paul Sale & Gary Tomlin.

Website – Rahul Varshney

Dedicated to Philip, Carole, & Beth Berry

ALSO AVAILABLE!

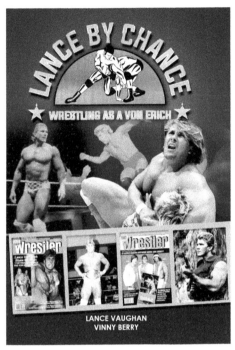

Read the story behind the creation of Lance Von Erich. Many believe that Lance was an established wrestler when he was discovered by World Class Championship Wrestling. Many think that he was brought into the sport because of Mike's illness with Toxic Shock Syndrome, and that Lance's career was over after Fritz and Kerry exposed his identity on television... Not true! Enjoy this candid look at the rise and fall of the World Class wrestling promotion and the man who carried the company's banner when the real Von Erichs could not.

WWW.WRESTLEVILLE.COM

REMEMBERING DAFFNEY

Jon-Paul Le Blanc - 4 Corners Photography

July 17, 1975 - September 1, 2021
NATIONAL SUICIDE PREVENTION LIFELINE
1-800-273-8255
suicidepreventiononline.org

Milton Keynes UK
Ingram Content Group UK Ltd.
UKHW021456080124
435669UK00025B/1175

9 798985 668407